My Affliction for His Glory is a [...]
bination of biblical truth and [...]
will find the gospel richly woven through the many inspiring, heartbreaking, and sometimes hilarious stories of Daniel's journey, in which he has learned to trust God and navigate life without arms. We are reminded that no matter what hand we have been dealt in life, that "our pain gives us a platform." And despite the numerous challenges, criticisms and opportunities to throw in the towel, Daniel's story is a platform which beautifully shows off the glory of Christ. No matter how difficult your life has been, you will be inspired and blessed by this book.

—Adam Ramsey, network director for Acts 29 Australia/
New Zealand, lead pastor of Liberti Church

Though this book may help overcome life's obstacles, that isn't what it's about. Ritchie redeems the often short-sighted genre of Christian Living with a gospel-saturated biography that covers many areas of the Christian life compressed into a very concise and entertaining read. Pastors, spouses, singles, males, females, adults and children alike will all be encouraged, as well as walk away with a renewed—or first time—laser like focus on the gospel message.

The words inside of this gospel-drenched book will impress you. The fact that they were all typed using toes will impress you even more. Ritchie has done more with his pinky toe than most will of us will ever do with both arms and their respectively connected hands.

—Timothy J. Trudeau, CEO of Syntax Creative;
GRAMMY-nominated producer; guest writer for Desiring
God, CCM Magazine, and Rapzilla

My Affliction for His Glory is a meaningful and stirring reflection on Christian faithfulness in the midst of life's trials. In it, Daniel Ritchie draws upon his experience of suffering to help us find our hope and Christ no matter how difficult the circumstances or deep the doubts. I enjoyed every moment of it and came away challenged in my walk with the Lord. Highly recommended.

> —Bruce Riley Ashford, provost and professor of theology & culture, Southeastern Baptist Theological Seminary; author of *Every Square Inch* and *One Nation under God*

I've known Daniel for many years and his life story is a testimony of the transformative power of the gospel and the resilience provided by Christ's indwelling Spirit. Reading Daniel's story will inspire you to never say never and to endeavor to accomplish difficult things. More importantly, Daniel's story will remind readers that grace is often the clearest when the days seem the darkest. I came away from reading *My Affliction For His Glory* with the incredible reminder that for the believer there is no such things as purposeless pain."

> —Dayton Hartman, lead pastor of Redeemer Church (Rocky Mount, NC); adjunct professor, Southeastern Baptist Theological Seminary; author of *Church History for Modern Ministry* and *Lies Pastors Believe*

Daniel's life is a powerful picture of what happens when a person embraces the sovereignty and purpose of God for his life. His journey has not been an easy one, but he brings both inspiration and personal conviction to anyone he meets and impacts. He has captured the power and essence of what God has done through him and in him in this book, and I have read and reread it and will use it for years to come to inspire, challenge, help, and grow believers and to share with unbelievers so that a clear picture of the gospel might be laid out and witnessed by a life that has been shaped by its power.

—Brody Holloway, cofounder and executive director of Snowbird Wilderness Outfitters; teaching pastor of Red Oak Church

Whenever I am asked about favorite sermon illustrations to use when speaking, I don't refer to some story or anecdote, but to a personal friend: Daniel Ritchie. Daniel is one of the most amazing Christians I've ever known. I am thrilled that his story is now in book form, because readers everywhere will benefit from the insights of one whose heart that has communed with the Lord for many years. I love the guy, but reading his book is deeply ... *convicting.* Which is exactly what the pampered church of the 21st-century needs. Get ready for God to deeply change you while reading *My Affliction for His Glory*, the story of one of God's champions, Daniel Ritchie.

—Alex McFarland, director of The Center for Apologetics & Christian Worldview, North Greenville University, South Carolina

If you're trying to make sense of your past, read this book. If you're trying to discern through the present, read this book. If you need wisdom on your next steps, read this book. Daniel Ritchie will help you understand that the path to navigating your unique calling is by first embracing this incredible spiritual truth—"My grace is sufficient for you, for my power is perfected in weakness" (2 Cor 12:9 CSB).

—Daniel Im, author of *No Silver Bullets*; coauthor of *Planting Missional Churches*; director of church multiplication at NewChurches.com

"Christ is better." I knew Daniel when he was a middle and high school student and watched him struggle into an embrace of these truths. It was, an is, a beautiful story that moves me to wonder and gratefulness. This story will show you that you are fearfully and wonderfully made and that your worth in Christ is far better than all the arms in the universe.

—J.D. Greear, pastor of Summit Church; author of *Gaining by Losing* and *Jesus, Continued...*

Daniel takes truth to struggle in this little book. He opens up about his own personal trials and wounds, but then points us to God's all-sufficient grace and wisdom. He reminds us to see ourselves rightly, through the lens of Scripture and through our identity in Christ, and not through the world's expectations and definitions of "the good life." His passion for the gospel also leads to some wonderful expressions of humility, and the call to boldly proclaim the gospel to others regardless of our current situation and context. His testimony will challenge you and encourage you in all these ways and more.

—Tony Merida, pastor for preaching, Imago Dei Church (Raleigh, NC)

Daniel embraces his earthly affliction with gratitude—not because it's easy or painless—but because he has fixed his eyes on our glorious Savior. I'm honored to endorse this book. If it affects readers a fraction as much as Daniel's life has affected me, they will walk away with a radically different outlook on life, having faith that there is no heartache, grief, or affliction too severe for our compassionate God.

—Phillip Holmes, director of communications, Reformed Theological Seminary

My Affliction for His Glory: Daniel's deep joy is at work in these pages, where the telling of his story points to the beauty of the Savior. This book is a winsome look at the love of God for His children and a call to rejoice that what He says about you is true: you are loved more than you let yourself believe.

—Mason King, spiritual formation pastor, The Village Church (Fort Worth, TX)

Daniel Ritchie's story is both inspiring and convicting. Ultimately, it is the story of the gospel itself. It is the story of how God alone gives us life and purpose. It is the story of how God's strength shows up most powerfully in our weakness. Whatever your affliction—and we all have them—this book will help you see it as an opportunity to serve and glorify God.

—Warren Smith, vice president of mission advancement, Colson Center for Christian Worldview

What an incredibly important story for our culture to embrace: our affliction gives God glory and is for our good. Daniel's story is absolutely beautiful, inspiring, challenging, and honest. I found myself mesmerized as he described his pain and struggle while still elevating the goodness and purposes of God. Daniel's story will make you love Jesus more and want to surrender all you have (no matter what) to chase after Him.

—Aaron Ivey, worship pastor, The Austin Stone

MY AFFLICTION FOR HIS GLORY

MY AFFLICTION FOR HIS GLORY

—

Living Out Your Identity in Christ

DANIEL RITCHIE

KIRKDALE PRESS

My Affliction for His Glory: Living Out Your Identity in Christ

Copyright 2018 Daniel Ritchie

Kirkdale Press, 1313 Commercial St., Bellingham, WA 98225
KirkdalePress.com

Print ISBN 9781683590828
Digital ISBN 9781683590835

Kirkdale Editorial: Abigail Stocker, Eric Bosell, Sarah Awa
Cover Design: Brittany Schrock
Typesetting: Beth Shagene

Heather,
what a gift you are to me!
I may not be wise or clever enough
to put it into words, but you are
a true measure of grace.

Contents

My Life Is His Story

I'll never graduate.

I'll never amount to anything.

I'll never find someone to spend my life with.

I'll never do anything that matters in the
    long run.

"Never" is a word I've heard a lot in my life. Having been born without either of my arms, I spent the first few years of my life being told all the things that I would never be able to do. I remember my mom saying, "Everything doctors said started to seem less like professional opinions and more like prophecies of doom." In their professional opinion, I was a lost cause. I was too broken.

One "never" builds on another that builds on another— and eventually you buy the lie that you will never succeed, that you will never amount to anything. For much of my life I faced the battle in my heart that I was going to live up to the doomsday prophecies that my doctors offered. For a time, I was convinced they were right. It was going to be far too difficult to make my feet do what hands were meant for. A man with no arms was never going to fit in a world where everyone has two arms.

But God had more in store for me than to be a victim of a life defined by the things that I was never going to be. In the genius way He crafted me, I learned to do the everyday tasks meant for hands with my feet: brushing my teeth, combing my hair, fixing a bowl of cereal or even making my morning coffee. The things I was told I would never do—walk, eat, dress myself, live independently—I now do with ease.

I pray that my story will allow you to see that God does not operate according to human logic. The Scriptures are littered with people who never should have found a way out of their circumstances: Joseph, Moses, David, Ruth, Job, and Paul were all people who should have been defeated by the enormities they all faced. Yet, God triumphed in the lives of each of these people. God doesn't say "never."

Some of you may come away from this book inspired by what I was able to overcome. If that is you, I thank God for that. But without God and His redemption, I would still be a victim of my perceived inadequacies. I would still feel hopeless, unlovable, and despondent—much like I was before Christ rescued me as a teenager. It is that rescue that makes this book possible—and your rescue, too. I pray that you will rest in the same grace that I've received by the time you finish this book.

If anything sticks with you after you finish this book, I pray it is this: Christ is better. He is better than your sin. He is better than any of your relationships. He is better than your most glorious victories or your darkest defeats.

Surrendering my life to Him was the sweetest victory that I have ever tasted. Nothing is better than knowing I have been adopted by Christ to do His work and that I can trust my life to a perfect Heavenly Father. I pray that is true for you as well—may the pages of this book help you taste and see that the Lord is truly good.

Ultimately, this book is a gospel book. I offer many stories in these pages: each story is evidence of God's grace and movement in my life. Even in the times when I had not yet claimed Christ as my Lord, God was working through each joy and each heartbreak. I might have the most visible part in each story, but the story I am telling is His story. This is about His grace, His strength, and His sovereign hand. This is His book.

CHAPTER 1

Born with Purpose

"Do you want us to let him go?"

Those were the ominous first words that greeted a newborn boy as he entered this world. His birth was not a moment of joy. It was a moment of heartbreak and fear. He was supposed to be born healthy. Instead he was born without arms and he was not breathing on his own. In the delivery room doctor's opinion, it was hopeless. In view of suffering and pain that certainly waited for him in the future, the little boy's life was not worth saving.

A harsh stillness swept over the delivery room after the doctor belted out those seven brutal words. Each word landed with the weight of an elephant on the hearts of the two parents in the delivery room that day. Their hearts broke. Their minds raced. *Is this really happening? Why us? Can we even get through something like this?* An entire room waited for an answer.

"Do whatever it takes. Save my son."

Those were the only words that a stunned father could croak out. In the blink of an eye this little boy was rushed to another room across the hall where busy doctors and nurses fought to bring a boy back to life. Yet in the delivery room, there was only a painful quiet as two parents were left to themselves. The young couple grabbed each other's hands. They wept and they prayed. As fear and pain choked away most of their words, they offered up a simple prayer: "God, if you let our little boy live, we will give him over to You." Their prayer was simple in light of such sorrow. But this was bigger than them, and they knew it.

Seconds scraped by as this couple waited for any news of their baby boy. When the longest fifteen minutes of their life had crawled by, a nurse walked in holding a wiggling baby boy. The doctors had brought this little boy back to life. The boy who had entered the world with a stunned silence was now cooing with joy in the arms of his relieved parents. In one of the most desperate times imaginable, God answered the humble prayer of two parents.

That was the prayer of my parents, and that lifeless, armless baby boy was me. Harry and Emily Ritchie are my dad and mom, and they are my heroes. They stood strong in the face of a soul-crushing trial. As doctors saw no room for hope, my parents laid their hope on the Maker of the heavens and the earth. On the Maker of their little armless boy. Their faith was simple and unadulterated. As the author of Hebrews says, "Now faith is the assurance of things hoped for, the conviction of things not seen" (Hebrews 11:1). They had no certainty of hope for their little boy and had no vision for what lay ahead, but they trusted this moment to the loving Father they had already surrendered their lives to.

—

Two different worldviews were on a collision course that day in the delivery room: the view of the doctor that said my life was not worth it and the view of Christ that said my life was worth dying for. Of course, this was not the first time these worldviews butted heads. Even the gospels contain a glimpse of this debate in John 9 as Jesus and the disciples stumble across a man who was born blind:

> As he passed by, he saw a man blind from birth. And his disciples asked him, "Rabbi, who sinned, this man or his parents, that he was born blind?" Jesus answered, "It was not that this man sinned, or his parents, but that the works of God might be displayed in him." (John 9:1–3)

The disciples assumed that the blind man was the result of a mistake. Surely, this man was born blind because something went wrong. They were certain that this man's disability was the product of the disaster of sin. Yet, in the eyes of Christ, the man's disability was the product of the beauty of design. He was made like this for a reason. He was born blind for the glory of God, even though the disciples could not see that. And truthfully, I don't know if even the blind man saw the complete hope of God's plan for his life at the time. So as the grace of Jesus intersected with this blind man in the gospel of John, one man was about to see his life changed and an entire town was about to be shaken by the work of God in this man's life.

In healing the blind man, Jesus displayed to the world the life and the power that He truly was. This ex-blind man was now an eager disciple who proclaimed the power and grace of God to anyone in town who was willing to listen. The man who was once a powerless, blind beggar was now powerfully proclaiming the remarkable grace of God to anyone who would listen. God was using a blind beggar who had largely been forgotten by his town to proclaim His power. God had fearfully and wonderfully crafted this man with blindness so that God's power could be displayed in his life.

That is the reality of the gospel and the hope for the world. When the rest of the world sees hopelessness and frustration, the gospel proclaims fear-shattering hope and redemption. Our lives are never defined by the circumstances of our birth or upbringing. God's purpose and value are stamped on our lives long before we take our first breath. The Father calls every baby in the womb a precious life, and that remarkable value carries through to the grave. You are not defined by your greatest weakness or most recent failure. The gospel of God's grace bids us to define our worth by what He says and not by the shame of our failure or the pain of our burdens.

It was through the lens of the gospel that Jesus viewed the blind man that day. He was not the sum of his unfortunate circumstances; he was a remarkable vessel of grace in the marvelous, mud-soaked hands of the Savior. The grace of Christ triumphs in every circumstance—even in the deepest possible suffering.

That is the worldview that my parents anchored themselves to—God is sovereign in all things. Even as a hushed fear rushed over the delivery room that day, God was not fearful. He was not surprised. He was not overwhelmed by the magnitude of my health problems. He admired His handiwork. He rejoiced over the son whom He had fearfully and wonderfully made. When fear was wrecking those hearts the day I was born, and as doctors wondered if there could ever be a future for my independent life, God was steadfast. He made His perspective clear through the psalmist:

> For you formed my inward parts;
>   you knitted me together in my mother's womb.
> I praise you, for I am fearfully and wonderfully made.
> Wonderful are your works;
>   my soul knows it very well.
> My frame was not hidden from you,
> when I was being made in secret,
>   intricately woven in the depths of the earth.
>
> (Psalm 139:13–15)

Every single bit of who we are is carefully crafted by the Father. Eyes, hair, nose, ears, teeth, toes, arms—or the lack thereof—are beautiful brush strokes in our personal canvas that God has painted. He did not make mistakes or leave us lacking. He gives grace and purpose to all of us from the moment we are conceived. He has molded and shaped our bodies and set forth our days even before a name was thought for us.

My parents' faith would be tested over the next few weeks and months as my parents ran me through a gauntlet of pediatricians and orthopedic doctors in an attempt to get a game plan for what lay ahead. At each doctor's appointment, my parents were greeted by another dark prognosis. *Daniel will never write. Daniel will never walk well. Daniel will never be able to feed himself. Daniel will never be an independent adult.* My mom and dad felt like they were being crushed to death with the picture the doctors were painting about what was to come. They could not help but to feel unqualified to bear the brunt of such a trial. Yes, even as they absorbed blow after blow of bad news, they fought on and never once had a thought of giving up on me.

I thank God for giving me the parents that He did. As doctor after doctor only saw me as a baby who had little hope, my parents saw me as a gift from God—a fearfully and wonderfully made image bearer of his Creator—who just happened to be born without arms. Even in my disability, I reflected my Heavenly Father. No bit of bad news or discouragement would shake my dad and mom off the fact that I was a perfect creation in the hands of a perfect Creator. God defined the precious value of my life even when my delivery room doctor saw little room for value or hope. God had woven together the baby that Harry and Emily had waited for. God had revived the lifeless baby they had prayed for that day in the delivery room. God would define the preciousness, hope, and future for the baby God had blessed them with.

God was prepared for what lay ahead, and He would work all things together for good—to those who trust Him. That single premise of trusting in God was set to be my greatest struggle over the next fifteen years. Attempting to trust God as my trials and frustrations swirled around me was creating resentment deep in my heart.

The Lies We Buy

As I grew up, my parents continued to see me as a vessel of God's grace, but I had a completely different perspective of myself. I saw myself as broken. I would watch my friends play spring baseball while I could only sit in the stands and watch. My classmates would climb the monkey bars while I stayed grounded. Guys on the basketball court could grab rebounds when balls would just bounce off my face. I was not like anyone in my entire school, and I hated it.

At one time or another we come to despise the things that make us stand out from the crowd. Every time someone points out a difference, it feels like someone is chucking a rock at us.

> You're too short.
> You're too fat.
> You talk funny.
> You're not smart enough.
> You don't have enough friends.
> You don't make enough money.

The deadly lie we buy into is that we are defined by what we do not have. The lie that I bought into was that I was hopelessly different. My identity was wrapped up in being armless, and there was not a single thing I could do to make my situation any better. I was chasing a hope that I knew I could never reach. I wanted to blend in. I wanted to look like everyone else. I wanted to be what I thought was "normal." To me, being different seemed like being sentenced to prison.

Yet, "different" was never meant to define who I am. It is Jesus who defines our identity and not the situations we are placed in or the choices that we chase after. It is the careful craftsmanship, grace, and purpose of Christ that are meant to give me identity and hope. I let my fear and my pride push me away from that true hope of the gospel. I had settled into accepting a lie of being different over the truth of being perfectly crafted—and it was wrecking my life.

All along the way, the truth of God's love for me was right in front of me, but I was reluctant to trust. I let my feelings of insecurity and hurt blind me to His grace and love. That blindness remained until I was fifteen, when I clearly saw God's love for me. This was not some sort of warm and fuzzy moment for me, but it was a moment of brokenness. The Father loved me as His perfect creation. He had a plan of hope for me. He lavished grace upon grace to me throughout the whole of my life. God had loved me even through every heartbreak and every frustration.

The brokenness came when I realized that God loved me at my worst. He loved me when I sulked at the body He had knit together with His own hands. He loved me as I turned my back to the blessings He had showered me with. He loved me when I hated Him for how my life had unfolded. He loved me even when I chose sin and disobedience over resting in Him. Paul expresses the state of my heart in Romans 5:10 when he says, "For if while we were enemies we were reconciled to God by the death of his Son, much more, now that we are reconciled, shall we be saved by his life."

All through my teenage years I battled against feeling like less than a whole person. No one else I knew had to eat every meal with his or her feet. No one else I knew got stared at like I did in public. I struggled to see God's love for me when I did not even love the person I was. Yet God used the weight of John 3 when I was fifteen years old to assure me that He truly loved me. I saw that the most horrific thing about my life was not my disability—it was my disobedience toward Him. He sent His Son to ransom me from the sin and shame I was intricately tied to. God's love for me was entirely evident in my deepest anguish. He pursued me even when I wanted nothing to do with Him. I broke down as I sat in my bedroom as a fifteen-year-old boy and looked at how God had taken all the steps to restore relationship with sinful man like me.

From minute one of my life, when my earthly father said, "Save him; that is my son," to this moment when my Heavenly Father said, "I want to adopt you as my son," God's love for me was living and active. That day I submitted to the lordship and love of Christ and His Spirit has not stopped transforming my wayward heart since that day.

Where anger, insecurity, and hatred once reigned in my heart, there was now a sense of peace. Certainty and love entrenched my heart. God had peeled back the layers of my fear and allowed me to wholly trust my life to Him. That is where the daily aspects of my life truly changed—when I trusted Jesus as the Lord of my whole life and not just the Savior for the eternity to come. In trusting my every step to Him, I did not need other people's opinions to validate my worth. I did not need to feel like everyone else because my

Abba did not make me like anyone else for a reason. Every day that I live is another day that I get to see my life as my Father sees it—precious, remarkable, vibrant, and beautiful.

Seeing the Right Image

Beyond seeing each day as precious, God was helping me to see the beauty of what He had crafted in my physical body. Grabbing hold of the truth that I had been made in God's image—the *imago Dei*—changed how I had once viewed what I thought was a broken body. The armless baby boy that God had formed in my mother's womb was a perfect masterpiece crafted by the One who crafted the created order. I stopped focusing on my flaws—having no arms—and started to see how God had graciously crafted me—from my talented toes to my flexible back. God had crafted me as a man who was to bear His very image to a watching world.

As my value was clearly seen, the purpose of my life was just as visible. Just as the blind man in John 9, all of us are fearfully and wonderfully made to put the glory of God on display. Being made as image bearers, we are meant to reflect the glory of the Father to the rest of the world. We will all have those who question our worthiness as image bearers, just as the disciples questioned the blind man's worthiness. Yet there is not one of us who is a lesser reflection of the Father than another. God did not make a misstep in making us as He did. We are all uniquely and deliberately fashioned for His glory. The uniqueness in each of us is not supposed to be a bad thing, but rather another beautiful facet through which the glory of God shines.

When I embraced the reality of God's glory being seen in my armlessness, the outlook of my everyday life shifted from burdensome to being full of blessings. Each person I met was no longer a potential critic but someone in need of seeing God's grace and love. I did not have to fear what people might say about me, because who I am in Christ is already secure. I did not have to depend on people's validation to be able to know that I am loved and that I am valuable. God already promised this, and His promise is not subject to what is happening around me. It is a steadfast promise. I do not have to prove myself for the Father to love. It is that secure promise that frees us up to live the life that God has granted us with peace and passion.

The security of love that God gives is a security that brings life and purpose to all of us. You do not have to cower and hide from your perceived inadequacies. God has created all of us with the tools to be used for His glory, and He has clothed us with what we need for the journey of life that is set before us—His righteousness, His strength, His joy, and His gospel. The Creator of you and me is also the author of life and the very One who gives our lives purpose. As we dwell securely in the weight of all of that, our lives are not filled with darkness and fear—but with light and purpose.

It was that purpose that would become the launching point for me. The purpose of declaring a glorious and creative God to a desperate world, which is a world that feels just as broken as I had once felt. As I began to mature in my faith, that is where the *imago Dei* drove me even deeper into a gospel-driven purpose. I am reminded of how deep and personal the reality of *imago Dei* is for every single person on the planet when I read about the persons of the Trinity speaking among themselves about man being made in God's image in Genesis 1:27: "So God created man in his own image, in the image of God he created him; male and female he created them." Knowing that God has fashioned each human in His image is a concept that the modern church has made deeply personal. *You* are made with purpose. *You* are to reflect the glory of *your* Creator. *You* are a flawless creation by the hands of our Creator God.

Those are all important truths to write on our own hearts. Yet the Christian must realize those truths also apply to the people you work with, to the people you hate, and to the unreached people group on the other side of the globe. All humankind is fashioned in His image. We are all designed to be reflectors of God's glory, and the entire planet needs to know that fact.

As we shift our understanding of being made in the image of God from being a strictly personal understanding to seeing that every human is made in the image of God, our hearts toward others change. As we see people as the craftsmanship of our Creator God, we are more likely to recognize their gifts and not their flaws. The *imago Dei* affects how we view the marginalized in society. When we see the orphan, the widow, the poor, the disabled, or the refugee as both fearfully and wonderfully crafted works of the Creator, it becomes more difficult to distance ourselves from those in need.

When we see all people as being created in the image of God, we won't get hung up on our differences. The dividing lines of culture, race, disability, or nationality are not an excuse for the believer to withhold love or the gospel from another person. There are scores of people in our lives who are different than us and who feel like strangers and aliens in this world. This is a sensation the believer knows well. We live in a world that we are not of, but we have been reconciled into a family of an untold number of brothers and sisters. It is the message of value and reconciliation of the gospel that we shine into a hurting world: "All this is from God, who through Christ reconciled us to himself and gave us the ministry of reconciliation" (2 Corinthians 5:18). We can't let the fear of our personal inadequacies or the fear of cultural differences keep us from sharing this message of reconciliation.

God has made us for more than fear—He has made us with purpose for His glory. We are not a mistake; we are wonderful. When we think we are lacking, God has freely given. When fear of the unknown and wondering was God's goodness arises, there is a certainty of the fullness of God's love for us. Do not submit to the uncertainty of your worthiness and value. God has written a beautiful story for you. Rest in knowing that God has made you without mistakes. He has *made* you—fearfully and wonderfully.

CHAPTER 2

Dependent on Him

"God don't make no junk."

That is a common phrase around the area where I grew up in North Carolina. People fired that phrase at me a lot when I was a kid. Most of the time I would shrug it off because deep down in my heart my insecurities would tell me otherwise. Every once in a while, that phrase would catch me in a good mood and I would stop and take note of how God had made me. Despite all the predictions by orthopedic and pediatric doctors about my lack of independence, God had designed me otherwise. God may have not given me arms, but he had given me two legs that were just as good.

Even from my infancy, I had an intuition to use my legs and feet in ways that people would ordinarily use their arms and hands. No one needed to teach me—it was as if God had written it on my heart. For instance, when most toddlers want you to pick them up, they will simply stick their arms up in the air. It is the universal sign for, "Hey, tall person, pick me up." There is no way I could get my point across like that, so I had to improvise. Whenever I wanted someone to pick me up, I would lie down on my back and stick my legs straight up in the air. Now, while this certainly led more than one person to believe I had just died, it worked to tell my parents that I wanted them to pick me up. Awkward but effective.

So many of the ways I devised to accomplish daily tasks could be summed up as just that: awkward but effective. However, getting to the place where I could be as effective as kids my age who had hands was incredibly difficult. Trying to make your feet do what no other person's feet could do was a challenge, but I was also flying blind. It wasn't like there was an Armless Anonymous group or a "How To" DVD on being armless. Learning simple things—using a spoon with my feet, putting on a shirt, coloring with crayons—was an exercise in trial and error. Many times, the only way I could learn came from watching how my parents did things with their hands, and I would try to emulate them with my feet.

The only drawback to the trial-and-error method is that there is a lot of trial and a lot of error. There were times when I could not make my toes and feet do what I wanted them to do. Other times there would be no good substitute for having a thumb or a wrist. I became well acquainted with failure and frustration. If something became too challenging I would do what any good person would do: I would quit. None of us particularly enjoys subjecting ourselves to failure over and over.

Small victories were what got me through an unrelenting stream of small problems. Yet, among the frustrations, the evidence of God's grace was very apparent to my mom and dad. God had given me everything I needed, including a very capable body and a dynamic duo of parents, for me to thrive in everyday life. My battle was not a matter of being able but a matter of being willing. I would get dejected at the constant pain of failure. I would be exhausted by having to try so hard for what people with hands could do with ease. My body was willing, but my heart was weak.

I Can Because He Does

If there is one thing that most people do not enjoy, it is having to work hard, and I was no different. My parents are loving and affectionate, but they knew that coddling me and doing everything for me was going to be the worst thing for my long-term independence. Their deepest desire was to be my greatest advocates but to also be a driving force for me to keep fighting.

My parents made it house rule that I could never utter the phrase "I can't." They viewed it on the same level as a cuss word in our house. Whenever things would get hard for me, I would inevitably fire off, "Mama, I can't do this." Every time I said that phrase, the hair on the back of my neck would stand up because I knew what was coming. Sometimes it was timeout. Sometimes I would be grounded if I was especially whiny. It may seem to be heartless, but it was creating a resolve in my heart. Through my parents' faithfulness and God's graciousness, there was a never-giving-up resolve that was beginning to bubble up inside of me.

Menial tasks were unbelievably difficult for me. Something as simple as carrying my toys around the house was an impossible task. I could carry one car at a time from room to room in my mouth. I was getting tired of the metallic aftertaste! But resolve and creativity were two powerful assets that God gave me in my early life.

One day when I was four years old, I started looking for a better answer. I tore my room apart looking for something that was going to help me out. As I dug everything out of my closet floor, I spotted my Easter basket. As I began to look over the basket, I realized that I could stick my head through the handle on the basket and it would dangle from my neck. I had found the perfect way to get my toys from point A to point B. My new way to carry my cars around meant I would put the basket on the floor, load the cars in the basket, stick my head through the handle, and be on my way.

As I started kindergarten, my single goal was to do everything my classmates did. I wanted to be a part of a regular class, to do all the assignments they did and to climb on the monkey bars with all my friends. The one bonus I had going for me was that I didn't have to worry about falling off the monkey bars and breaking my arm.

One thing that was important to me was to have my own desk in my class just like everyone else did. The desks in our class were the kind where the desk and chair came in two separate pieces. This meant I could slide my chair a good bit back from the desk so I could have enough room to put my feet on top of the desk and write and color. This setup worked okay for a time, but I started having some problems. My feet were probably sixteen inches above my hips for long periods of time. This started causing cramps in my quadriceps and hamstrings that were almost debilitating. My goal of being like everyone else in this little kindergarten kingdom was starting to slip away.

In stepped my ever-creative and resilient dad. He was a diesel mechanic and salesman by day and a Mr. Fix-It by night. He had a MacGyver-like ability to fashion anything out of duct tape, a soda bottle, and a paper clip. For him, the desk situation was fixable. One day he stopped by my school to see how he could make a desk work for his son. He stood quietly in my kindergarten class at Nathaniel Greene Elementary scanning this desk for any signs of adaptability.

After a couple of minutes, he walked out to his truck and came back into the classroom with a Phillips screwdriver. He flipped the desk on its top and went to work. My dad had seen that the desk legs had come in two pieces that were joined together by a single screw. My dad took the screw out and then removed the bottom part of the leg, lowering the table by at least a foot. Flipping the table back on its legs, my dad asked me to give the new setup a try. I plopped in my chair and started coloring. It worked perfectly. My hips and feet were nearly parallel with each other. No more straining to write, and no more leg cramps. It was a small victory but a victory nonetheless.

My parents would constantly remind me, "I can do all things through Him who strengthens me." At that point in my childhood I was not a believer, so I know I did not fully grasp the weight of the verse. However, I do remember thinking to myself, "God has made me for greater things than quitting." It was in those times that my dad and mom were carefully sowing the seeds of the gospel into my life. The one sentence that kept trailing off the lips of my parents was not just a random sentence, but a verse of Scripture.

Later, that single passage, Philippians 4:13, would become the anthem of my early Christian life. Yet, as an unbelieving kid, I would readily quote this single Scripture whenever when I felt like the chips were stacked against me. This verse had become a sort of battle anthem for me in dealing with frustration and trials.

It wasn't until years later, when I was a Christian, that I knew I was missing the full picture of what the Holy Spirit was saying through Paul in that verse. One day I sat down with a journal, my study Bible, and my mom's commentary on the book of Philippians so that I could better understand the verse that had become my life verse. I wanted to fully understand the strength that I had in Christ.

As I started to dig into God's Word, the Holy Spirit started to transform me with the weight of these few verses. One of the first things that God taught me was that the power of verse 13 takes on more weight when you read it in view of the two verses before it:

> Not that I am speaking of being in need, for I have learned in whatever situation I am to be content. I know how to be brought low, and I know how to abound. In any and every circumstance, I have learned the secret of facing plenty and hunger, abundance and need. I can do all things through him who strengthens me. (Philippians 4:11–13)

I had made the verses simply about being a better me, but the verses were about resting in a glorious God.

The world had taken these verses and slapped them onto T-shirts, coffee mugs, and motivational posters. When we want to be a better boss or crank out one more set at the gym, we rattle out Philippians 4:13. We tell ourselves, "I can do this!"

Is there a more misquoted verse in the Bible? We take it out of context and apply it to our lives so we can be better employees, students, athletes, or just better people. But that is not the point of the Scripture here. This isn't a testimony of someone who is constantly successful. It is instead the testimony of a man who has Christ and has found Him as his source of joy, hope, and strength regardless of good circumstances.

There were times when small victories took the shape of having fun at the expense of my disability. Being incredibly adaptable allowed me to find things that I could do that few others could. One gift of using my legs for everything was that I had unreal flexibility. I could put both legs behind my head so that I could be a human pretzel. I could contort my body in ways that few others could. This allowed me to hide in tight places, like a cardboard box or toy chest, so that I could pop out and scare people. It was a fun advantage that my disability gave me.

That sort of perspective is what fueled me to enjoy the circumstances God had given to me instead of languishing in my disability. While having no arms kept me from doing some daily activities, it also allowed me to do things that no one else could do. I had to recognize that my difference and disability was not a curse but a gift.

That sort of mindset rings true in almost any trial that we must endure. If we see the trial before us as an unfair burden, we will most certainly crumble under the weight of it. What if we saw every trial and challenge as a gift by which God can push, pull, and mold us into the person He desires? In that perspective we can push through, resting in God's strength, knowing that God is working in our life even in the smallest moments. In these steps of faith, we can push through all sorts of fear and doubt.

In my late elementary school years, my friends and I would try to find ways to push my limits even beyond what I thought I could. One of my lifelong friends, Andy, always wanted to find things that I had never done but that I "needed" to do. I had never shot a BB gun, so he showed me how. I assumed it was impossible for me to throw a baseball, until the day we gave it a try. I had never tried ice skating until he convinced me that I could do it. We even tried to figure out ways for me to play hockey—which never worked out well, but we had fun trying.

I grew up in the middle of the country in North Carolina. The joke in Julian, the town I grew up in, was that cows outnumbered people in our town two to one. It may have been a joke, but I am convinced it is true. In a tiny country town like that, two kids had to make their own fun if they wanted to play anything at all. There were plenty of days when we went outside and made forts. We would play soccer in the back yard or street hockey in the driveway. Those were all fun ways to spend an afternoon, but they had gotten old as we did them day after day during the summer. We needed to take things to the next level.

So we invented go-kart Frisbee. That year Andy had gotten a go-kart, and he absolutely loved it. I had always been a little bashful about trying to drive it because I did not want to crash my buddy's new, awesome toy. I mean, who drives with their feet?

I do. I drive with my feet. At least that is what Andy convinced me I could do. One foot on the steering wheel and one foot on the gas, and we were off and running. The only minor issue was that the brake pedal was on the other side of the steering column from the gas pedal. Basically, I had no way to stop the go-kart without taking my foot off the steering wheel. I was fine with that. I grew up in NASCAR country, and who needs brakes?

Miraculously, I never actually crashed while figuring out how to drive it. Somehow, I had mastered armless go-kart racing in a single afternoon. Like anything with a couple of ten-year-olds, we soon became bored with the go-kart. We needed to spice things up a little. That's when we added a Frisbee into the mix.

Our idea was basically a game of fetch—except there were a go-kart and an armless kid involved. We set up in the front yard of my buddy's house so we could have plenty of room for our new game. Andy would throw the Frisbee as far as he possibly could. I would stomp the gas on the go-kart, track the Frisbee down ... and catch it with my teeth. I have no idea how we pulled it off. In fact, we got so good at go-kart Frisbee that it, like so many other things, became boring to us. I might have missed out on some fun as a kid, but these small moments gave me some great memories.

So much of my childhood was spent crashing through barriers and limitations placed by others and even the boundaries I placed on myself. Those limitations hovered over me solely because of assumptions, doubt and fears. I would never know the full extent of what I could do unless I challenged what my fear proclaimed. Only by crashing through a limitation could I know for certain what I could do. These steps of faith helped to nudge me in the right direction. It was a direction toward dependence on Christ and contentment in Him. Whether the limitations were overcome or not, He was still enough.

Content in Christ

Imagine your life. Do people want to hear you wax eloquent about God's love and grace while you drive a nice car and have a wardrobe that rivals a Hollywood socialite? No, people would want to punch you in the face. Even for those who live in earthly prosperity, struggling through fear, worry, doubt, and value is a part of everyday life. No one is immune from a troubled heart. There is not a single worldly thing or person that will ever bring you true satisfaction and contentment.

Contentment comes only from a wholehearted transformation that comes from Christ alone. That sort of transformation is most evident when we are under fire. A content heart and life, even during trials and frustrations, is a life that glorifies God alone because that contentment is not of this world. When you can find unending hope in Christ in the dark times of life, you have a life that shouts about God's grace. Find satisfaction, joy, and contentment in Christ alone and you will be able to weather the most violent storm. Find your contentment in Him and you will show others His grace lived out.

In times of unrelenting trial, we taste a grace and hope that can come only from Christ. We understand mercy and love unlike ever before. I could not help but think back to Paul's testimony he shares in 2 Corinthians:

> Five times I received at the hands of the Jews the forty lashes less one. Three times I was beaten with rods. Once I was stoned. Three times I was ship-wrecked; a night and a day I was adrift at sea; on frequent journeys, in danger from rivers, danger from robbers, danger from my own people, danger from Gentiles, danger in the city, danger in the wilderness, danger at sea, danger from false brothers; in toil and hardship, through many a sleepless night, in hunger and thirst, often without food, in cold and exposure. And, apart from other things, there is the daily pressure on me of my anxiety for all the churches. (2 Corinthians 11:24–28)

Paul isn't content because everything is going right. Paul is content in the worst moments imaginable because of the constant security of the hope in Christ! This is the anti-prosperity gospel. His hope isn't doing greater things, being richer, and having his best life now. His hope in this life was crucified on the cross and raised in the resurrected power of Jesus. Our contentment can never be seen, tasted, or touched—our contentment is not of this world.

Imagine if Paul never had those terrible things happen to him that were described in 2 Corinthians 11. Would Philippians 4:13 carry the same authority if Paul had only experienced a life of success and prosperity? No.

Contentment in Christ exists when the circumstances of our lives are secondary to the beauty and glory of Jesus Himself. Contentment and comfort in Christ result only when we see Him as our ultimate joy. It is by setting our affections on Him, His character, and His cross that we can have our hearts stably resting in Him. That's when we taste true contentment in seasons of grace and in the midst of heartache.

All of that is easy to say when we are at ease and enjoying prosperity. But how do I say "Christ is enough" when the world around me seems to be tearing apart at the seams? That is the hard work of quieting our lives enough to focus on God's character even when our circumstances lash out against us. It is the words of Psalm 62:5–7 that ring true here:

> For God alone, O my soul, wait in silence,
>   for my hope is from him.
> He only is my rock and my salvation,
>   my fortress; I shall not be shaken.
> On God rests my salvation and my glory;
>   my mighty rock, my refuge is God.

As we rest in Christ as our refuge, we must constantly preach to ourselves who He is. He is our hope. He is our rock and salvation. He is our glory. We must stake our confidence and contentment in Christ, on who He has revealed

Himself as in His promises and not by the claims of our hurts and fears. We must daily remind ourselves of His goodness and gracious redemption of us. It is that hope that we cling to when our lives fall to pieces. We can say He is enough because His gospel has already shown itself to be completely sufficient to save us from sin, wrath, and death.

We don't rest in what is to come; we rest in what He has already done. We don't rest in what we feel and experience; we rest in the Savior who does not change in character. As we navigate the pressures of life we can rest assured that He is with us, and that is all we need. Our hearts are in the best place when we seek His presence above our prosperity.

CHAPTER 3

Listening to the Right Words

"Are you cold?"

If I had a dollar for every time someone asked me that question, I'd be a contender for the title of Richest Man in the World. This question is one that I certainly understand. Most people do not expect to meet an armless man. When people cross my path for the first time, they are naturally going to assume that I have my arms tucked in my shirt because I am cold. Of all the questions that people can ask me, that is one that bothers me the least. It might be the least offensive way of trying to figure out, "Where are his arms?"

"Bear attack." That's usually my reply to people so that we can break the awkward silence. Once I watch legitimate fear wash over their face for a couple of seconds, I come back with, "Naw man, I am just playing. I was born without arms."

It is an instant icebreaker. We get the armless elephant out of the room and we can dive right into meaningful conversation. Think of it as the ultimate party trick, but all I have to do is stand there.

I have this type of conversation nearly every day. It illustrates the point that my disability is visible to even the most casual observer. A trip to the grocery store or coffee shop is never just a quick and easy trip. Some people stop and stare in amazement. Some people want to sit and talk. Some people ask if they can take a picture of me. Each encounter is a reminder that I am very different from other people.

There were plenty of times when people treated me in the most loving and compassionate ways. Yet there were moments, so many moments, that hurt me to think about even twenty years after the fact:

- When my parents and I were asked to leave a restaurant because I ate with my feet.

- When I wasn't allowed to play in a YMCA soccer game until I took my arms out of my shirt.

- Being told I could not get on theme park rides with my friends because I was an insurance liability.

- Getting frisked at the mall because a store owner thought I was keeping stolen merchandise under my shirt.

My goal in life was just to be like everyone else, but the only thing I could be reminded of was that I was not like everyone else. In fact, I was *never* going to be like everyone else. I was settling into the heartbreaking reality that this was going to be everyday life for me. I had nowhere to run.

Overcoming Fear of Others and Self

All through that period of brokenness in my life—from age six to fifteen—I just wanted a hope to cling to: that one day everything would be better. I was a church kid from my earliest years, but my awareness of the hope of the gospel only went about as deep as the Southern moralism of "Don't smoke, drink, chew, or go with girls that do" and that if I loved Jesus I wouldn't go to hell. I knew how to be a "good" church kid—but I didn't know how to have hope in this life and in eternity because of the work of Christ. I had no idea what it meant to find my sufficiency in Christ in my everyday life.

People are always watching you. They will talk about you behind your back. They will attack you. They will question your motives. They are waiting for you to slip up. There is the constant urge to be just like them. There is the knee-jerk reaction to lash out at them when they lack compassion for you. There is the tendency to turn your back on those who are not with you.

There are days when the reminders about how different I am are particularly painful. People's initial reaction can go a long way in revealing what is going on in someone's heart. There is the person who will stop and stare blankly for seconds on end. There is the guy who will walk up beside me at the grocery store, grab my shirt sleeve, and look down it to see if there are any arms there. There are the people who take pictures of me when I am eating at a restaurant with my wife. No doubt those pictures are being sent to their friends with less-than-flattering captions.

Then there are the people who say horrible things right to my face:

"Gross."
"Freak."
"Weirdo."
"Cripple."
"Did you escape from the circus?"
"There are places for people like you."

I wish these were examples that I made up just so I could stick them in a book, but they are not. Every single one of these phrases has been said to me at least once over the last four or five years. In a nation deeply divided over racial issues, this even further illustrates the fact that there is a part of our human nature that makes us wary of those who are different than we are. I am a lightning rod for this phobia of difference (xenophobia, for those of you who like Latin) because I am unlike any other person that I know.

Words broke me.

I can't even begin to count the number of times I would go somewhere with my parents and come home crying because of what someone said to me. It didn't matter where we went—the mall, the playground, school, or even church—I was fair game for people.

I hated going into public—and very soon I started to hate people. Meeting anyone new was another chance for an awkward conversation. For all the well-intentioned people who were around me to encourage, there was always one jerk. One thoughtless sentence would shatter my already broken self-image. I began to lash out at people who said hurtful things to me. Rarely did things ever get physical—I only got in a couple of fights (my fault) as a kid. I often lashed out verbally in anger.

Even at the happiest place on earth, Disney World, I was not insulated from someone reminding me how weird they thought I was. I was six years old when I went to Disney with my parents, and I had just started to feel the weight of how different I was. It was clear how different I was from every single happy person in this theme park. (Except Captain Hook—we had a bonding moment.)

On one of the days at the park, I went to go hold a seat for my parents while they went and got some ice cream for all of us. While I sat in the hot Florida sun, a boy only a couple of years older than me came up and started talking to me. It was not long before he noticed my empty sleeves and things began to spiral out of control. He kept asking me where my arms were, and he would not believe me when I told him that was how I was born. He'd grab my sleeves, trying to peek down them—certain he was going to catch me in a lie. I was starting to squirm with the discomfort from the whole situation and kept looking over my shoulder hoping my parents would come back.

"Liar," he said. "You're just a big liar."

"Liar," he whispered.

"LIAR!" he screamed.

I'd had enough. I was hurt. I was alone. I decided to give this boy more than he could handle.

"You really want to know what happened? I'll tell you the truth," I said as I stared into this kid's eyes. "I was at the zoo earlier this year," the boy nodding like he was really getting the scoop, "and I got too close to the polar bear exhibit. The bear reached up and dragged me into the exhibit. Before the zookeepers could get to me and help, the bear managed to rip both of my arms off. I almost died right there."

The boy could not have gotten quieter. What happened next was an image that I will never forget. I watched fear and pain wash over the boy's face, and he sprinted off crying to his parents. I laughed for a minute, thinking that I had really showed that guy why he should not mess with me.

I waited for a few more minutes for my parents to return. As I waited, the image of that kid's terrified face kept playing back in my head. I had never made anyone scared of me before. I had never responded to a person like that before. It was the first time I can remember trying to hurt someone with my words. In an instant I had become the very type of person I despised.

Emotional wounds are my greatest burden. They are the wounds that come from being different and people letting you know that you are different. I have always hated the idiom we'd all repeat as kids—"Sticks and stones may break my bones, but words will never hurt me." But this is simply not true. Words *do* hurt.

For as devastating as the years of my broken self-image were, God's love was as equally as devastating to my fear and self-doubt. I had always seen the love of God as a sort of passive, mushy thing. I had never really known the love of my King who rules and reigns in my life in the most loving and fatherly way conceivable. God's love and power conquered every horrific thing about me: my sin, my brokenness, my captivity to the words of others, my crippling fear, and my hatred toward people.

In reconciling me to Himself, God was stitching me back together in His grace. Even though God was not making those soul-crushing comments go away, He had something better for me. He gave me the foundation to stand on while the mess in my life tried to wash over me. He was showing me the beauty of building my life on His Son.

One of the greatest fear-shattering portions of Scripture is in Colossians 2:

> Therefore, as you received Christ Jesus the Lord, so walk in him, rooted and built up in him and established in the faith, just as you were taught, abounding in thanksgiving. See to it that no one takes you captive by philosophy and empty deceit, according to human tradition, according to the elemental spirits of the world, and not according to Christ. For in him the whole fullness of deity dwells bodily, and you have been filled in him, who is the head of all rule and authority. (Colossians 2:6–10)

While Paul is tackling the heresy that was rampant in the Colossian church, the same truth rings true in our self-obsessed idolatry. The amazing gospel of Jesus is for our justification and for our sanctification. Our eternal life exists because of Him, and so our earthly life should be built on Him.

Paul goes on to say in the next chapter of Colossians that we cannot look to earthly things to be what fulfills us. We set our vision and our hearts on the One who is above and on nothing else. Christ is the One in whom we have "been filled." He is our everything in regard to salvation and life itself. He is the source of our joy (John 15:11), our strength (Philippians 4:13), our hope (1 Peter 1:3), our peace (Romans 5:1), and the basis for our very lives (Romans 11:36). That's what it is to find our sufficiency in Christ alone; it is when I anchor every meaningful part of who I am in Christ alone.

Carried in our Weakness

It is by building my life on what He has called me to and wrapping my heart with what He has said about me that I am sustained as I walk through this world. This is the only way I can stand in the face of unthinkable trials and the only means by which I can overcome the avalanche of human criticism that is bound to come my way.

The weight of being different has been the single greatest burden I have had to bear in my life. It has nothing to do with my physical disability and the burden that it brings on my body. I can do anything that another grown man can do with his hands. There is not a second of my life where I feel physically limited just because I am missing two limbs.

It is when I stake my life on Christ alone that I am able to withstand the pressures of being different. Yet, the moment I anchor my life in Christ, I am instantly different than the rest of the world. I no longer think like the rest of the world. I do not chase after the things that the world wants. I do not find my security in things that moth or rust can destroy. The believer is set free from the pressures of the world while, at the same time, becoming different than the world. The believer must take comfort in being set apart from the rest of this world.

This is seen in the prayer that Jesus prays over His disciples in John 17:

> I have given them your word, and the world has hated them because they are not of the world, just as I am not of the world. I do not ask that you take them out of the world, but that you keep them from the evil one. They are not of the world, just as I am not of the world. Sanctify them in the truth; your word is truth. As you sent me into the world, so I have sent them into the world. (John 17:14–18)

Jesus' prayer and mission for us is to go into a world that we are nothing like for the sake of the gospel. Jesus draws the clear line of difference between the world and His disciples, but He also prays that we remain here—as strangers and aliens. As I consider my past, I can say with certainty that being different than the rest of the world is a tough burden to bear. The call to be "in" but not "of" is a difficult call to accept ... but it is part of the role of being a disciple. It should not come as a surprise that our relationship with Christ will cost us something. Jesus reminds His disciples in Luke 14 that discipleship comes at a high price:

> Whoever does not bear his own cross and come after me cannot be my disciple. For which of you, desiring to build a tower, does not first sit down and count the cost, whether he has enough to complete

it? Otherwise, when he has laid a foundation and is not able to finish, all who see it begin to mock him, saying, "This man began to build and was not able to finish." (Luke 14:27–30)

Jesus uses the picture of a man building a tower to remind the disciples of what they are stepping into. In talking about the man building that tower, Jesus asks His disciples, "Does he not sit down and count the cost?" Any sane builder is going to sit down and see if he has what he needs to finish the task in front of him.

It is this sort of treatment from the world that few believers are prepared for. It is the burdensome weight of being a light in a dark place that causes so many people to wither in their faith. That is why we must count the cost of discipleship beforehand. When the weight of discipleship comes, we can stand because we are resting in the strength God gives.

Christ is sufficient—not my self-worth and not the praise of humans. As I build my life on Him alone and rely on His daily sustaining grace, Christ becomes my greatest motivation. I don't need to find comfort with this world or solace in the words of people because Jesus is my comforting shepherd and He alone speaks words worth listening to. His sufficiency allows me to count up the costs of following Him and to still be able to say, "He is worth it."

Do we do that as believers? Did we count the cost when we called Christ our Lord and Savior? I have to know that bearing my cross every day means I have died to everything this world offers me. I have to grasp the fact that if the world hated the Savior who healed the blind and lame, it will undoubtedly hate a person like me. The moment that we begin to talk about the gospel to the world, we are going to be branded as fools.

In Christ you are different, but He was different than this world too. People's words can cut like a knife, but the Word of God is a balm to my broken heart. There will be plenty of days when you feel painfully inadequate, but the sufficiency of Christ carries us in our weakness. You are going to feel different than this world, but so did our Lord. My prayer for you is that you would carefully count the cost of following Jesus and keep chasing Him because you know He is bigger and better.

CHAPTER 4

My Pain Is a Gift

"People aren't there to hear you—they want
to hear about God's grace in your life."

It was not long after I was saved at fifteen years old that
people wanted me to share my testimony with them. First,
I shared my testimony with my Sunday school class at
church. Then it was other adult Sunday school classes
who invited me to come and share. Then I got to speak
in front of my youth group of over one hundred students
at Pleasant Garden Baptist Church. These opportunities
were seemingly coming out of nowhere, and it made very
little sense to me. I was talking about the same saving grace
that ransoms every Christian. It was the same Lord who
conquered my sin and my insecurity. I had nothing to say
beyond what any pastor has ever said in a pulpit. There
was not a whole lot that I said that was out of the ordinary.

I felt completely out of my league when I stepped in
front of a group to share. I always thought that there was
someone more intelligent or more charismatic who could
be doing what I was doing. My ever-faithful mom reminded
me often: "People aren't there to hear you—they want to

hear about God's grace in your life." She was right in so many ways. The way I was communicating to a crowd was not terribly deep or witty. It was simply the recounting of God's grace in my wayward life that resonated with people. My two vacant sleeves were the proof of why I should hate God, but my words centered on His love for me. People wanted to see and hear this walking contradiction in person.

Very soon, the requests to hear my testimony grew past the walls of my own church. My very first time sharing my testimony in another church was because of a guy named Tracy. I had met Tracy the year before when he came to preach to my youth group, and we had talked after the meeting. We talked a lot about Jesus and our testimonies. He decided that he wanted me to speak to his students at First Baptist Church in Rock Hill, South Carolina.

Tracy invited me to speak at a New Year's Eve lock-in on the night of Y2K. On top of the fear of the world coming to an end, I had my own reservations about the night. I had refused the first time he had asked. There was no way that I was going to speak to a couple hundred students whom I had never met. My fear of crowds and their potential judgmental comments came crawling back into my mind. I was certain I could not possibly stand in front of that many people and not have one person mock me. My fear was stirring up an excuse for me to say no.

It was in that moment when the Holy Spirit started to remind me of the many truths that I had been sharing in my own church. I talked about being able to "do all things through Christ" and that "Christ is sufficient to pull anybody out of their mess." I had done quite a bit of talking about God's life-altering power, but was I living like it? It was time for me to walk the walk. I picked up the phone and called Tracy. "We'll see you New Year's Eve," I told him.

Two amazing things happened that night: the world did not end as people feared, and God got me through sharing my testimony in front of several hundred students. After I finished speaking, I considered it a small victory that I didn't throw up or pass out in front of a crowd that large. As I sat and reflected for a moment when I had finished, I really did wonder what people thought. Had I been clear enough to get my point across?

As the event ended, people started to come up and thank me for coming down and sharing. People spoke of how they related to the hurt I had gone through, even though they had arms. Teens would talk about how they were able to pay complete attention for the twenty minutes I spoke even though their normal attention span was five minutes. Affirming comments kept coming, person after person, that night. As the room emptied, I sat and talked with my dad. It was then that I first realized that God had given me a remarkable gift.

Strength in Weakness

Wherever I go, I get a steady diet of questions from people:

> "Where are your arms?"
> "Can you shave?"
> "How do you brush your teeth?

"Does someone have to help you eat?"

"How did you put your shirt on?"

"Can you drive a car?"

These are the questions that I most often hear from people who are meeting me for the first time. I can understand the thinking behind each question. If we are all honest with ourselves, it is not like we meet an armless guy every day. It is hard for people to envision how I do everyday tasks with my feet. I do not resent people like that, but I am grateful that people care enough to ask the things that their curiosity prompts.

Often these weighty questions stir emotions in my heart from the pain in my past. Questions like, "Was it hard being different than all your friends growing up?" or "Did you get picked on a lot as a little kid?" are queries that bring about meaningful conversation.

Yet there is one question that I am never surprised that people ask: "If you could go back in time and choose to have arms, would you do it?"

What's my surprising answer?

No.

I would not go back just so I could change the way God designed me. I understand that "no" is an easy two-letter word for me to fire off considering where God has led me now. At various points in my life, there is no doubt that I would have answered that question very differently. In my early teenage years, when I wrestled with my self-image, I would have quickly chosen to change the appearance that I hated so deeply.

Coming to grips with how God had fearfully and wonderfully crafted me was not an easy road to walk. Every day when I walk into the bathroom I am greeted with a reflection in the mirror of a man who has two empty sleeves. It is my daily reminder that I do not look like every person that I pass on the street. I do not fit in. I am different.

Being different than everyone else you know is an uneasy weight to carry. Wouldn't my life be easier if I looked like everyone else? I need to have arms like everyone else, right?

Choosing to have arms was not only a hypothetical question for me either. Just before I was to start kindergarten, the Shriners generously offered to fully fund robotic, full-arm prosthetics. The estimated cost of a surgery with prosthetics like that was hovering around $250,000. But the drawbacks to getting robotic prosthetics were tremendous. Technology today is lightweight and highly functional, but the robotic arms twenty-five years ago were clunky and had very limited capability. I could do almost any task with my feet faster than what the prosthetics could do. Secondly, the surgery was going to be like hitting the reset button on my development. I was going to have to re-learn how to do everything with my prosthetics that I had already conquered with my feet. The learning curve and recovery from surgery would have meant holding me back from starting kindergarten for a year while I caught up to the basic skills of my peers.

I sat down with my parents to try to decide what path we were going to send my life down. We listed the positives and negatives. We prayed about it. We even cried over it.

Our decision came down to a question of appearance or function. Was looking like everyone else in the world worth not being as functional as I already was with my feet? In the end, we were humbled by the generosity of the Shriners, but we decided it just was not the right move.

That might be the best decision I have ever made. Outside of being rescued and redeemed in Christ, being born without arms is the best thing that has ever happened to me. God fearfully and wonderfully making me has given me a voice in people's lives that I could not have otherwise. People have a deep sense of curiosity toward what it is like to be armless. People want to hear my story.

Giving Thanks Through Pain

Through all the pain, I've come to believe this: being born without arms is a gift from God.

It is with this bizarre gift that I could grab people's attention. People would instantly relate with my weakness, and all I had to do was to stand up. My difference was the ultimate attention grabber. As soon as I had people's attention I could answer the question that would pop up in people's mind, "How did he overcome all of this?" It was with their full attention that I could answer that question. It wasn't a matter of how I overcame anything; it had everything to do with how God gave the strength, purpose, and hope for me to press on.

It is my pain that I am thankful for, which is easy for me to say now. Yet I know that the first half of my life and all the frustration that came with it have reaped a bounty

I never could have produced on my own. God stepping in and carrying me along in my weakness has allowed me to taste His strength, grace, and love in such a robust way. My pain has magnified so many of His attributes.

I have always been drawn to C. S. Lewis, who tasted pain in ways that few can completely relate to. He lost his mother at an early age, was emotionally abandoned by his father, suffered from a respiratory illness as a teenager, fought in World War I, where he was wounded, and finally had to bury his beloved wife. Lewis wrote about such heartache in *The Problem of Pain*:

> Pain insists upon being attended to. God whispers to us in our pleasures, speaks in our conscience, but shouts in our pain: it is His megaphone to rouse a deaf world.

It is in our suffering that we are most keenly aware of God and His character. It is when our self-sufficiency is peeled away that we see how weak we really are. It is in that moment of weakness that, as Paul says in 2 Corinthians 12:9, His "power is made perfect in weakness." It is in our pain that God has us taste His power most intimately.

I see the reality of Lewis's statement quite clearly in my own life. God has shouted to me through my pain to remind me of His truth in many ways. As the mocking words of men fell on my heart like an avalanche, God showed me that it is only His words that bring life. It was in my brokenness that I saw God's true strength as He carried me along. It was in seeing my shattered identity as a disabled boy that I could see the beauty of being a blood-bought son. God used my hurt so that He could clearly write the lessons of His grace on my heart.

One of the most interesting realities of suffering is that our personal pain also speaks to those around us. Our pain becomes God's megaphone to a watching world around us. The world gravitates to the cancer patient who has hope and peace. Bystanders are astounded over the parents who cling to the Good Father as they bury their own child. My friends are taken aback when I can shrug off hateful words about my disability and turn my focus to what God says about me.

Our pain gives us a platform. The question becomes "What am I saying to the world in the midst of my pain?" Do I allow my faith to become the product of my circumstances, or is God still good even if my circumstances are not? The scope of His character and grace does not change when suffering comes. As I trust God, even in my heartache, I let my life speak of a hope that extends well beyond what we can see or touch. We reveal a glorious God who has better things than just these earthen vessels we get to live in. It points to the treasure inside that endures far beyond the reaches of what harm moth or rust can do.

As we suffer and trust, we taste a comfort from the Father that is distinct and true. It is in the fact that we know God is still reigning whether we taste comfort or affliction. In 2 Corinthians 1:3–6, Paul writes:

> Blessed be the God and Father of our Lord Jesus Christ, the Father of mercies and God of all comfort, who comforts us in all our affliction, so that we may

be able to comfort those who are in any affliction, with the comfort with which we ourselves are comforted by God. For as we share abundantly in Christ's sufferings, so through Christ we share abundantly in comfort too. If we are afflicted, it is for your comfort and salvation; and if we are comforted, it is for your comfort, which you experience when you patiently endure the same sufferings that we suffer.

It is the comfort that Christ brings us that we are now given to share with a hurting world. It is our pain that produces a ministry of comfort that we can walk in. His grace to us is meant to be displayed and not hidden by our silence. As our pain shouts to a hurting world, may our lives always sing of the fact that God is glorious even when our circumstances are not.

The Worst Thing Is the Best Thing

Opportunities to testify to God's grace in my life seem to come in bunches. I can go a couple of days and not really share my testimony with anyone. Then the next day I will be able to share with two or three different people. I don't have to ask people if they would like me to share my testimony—many people will ask me. God has given me an incredibly unique tool with regard to evangelism.

It is my lack of arms that opened the door for me to do all of this. God had given me a platform just by how He had made me. It gave me an instant magnetism in group settings, but it also spawned gospel conversations in ways

I never could have anticipated. Daily errands will almost always create enough curiosity in a person that they want to know how I do what I do. It might be me unloading a grocery cart by standing on one leg and putting groceries on the conveyor belt with the other foot. It might be the instant I slide a debit card out of my shoe, swipe it in the machine, and punch in the PIN with my big toe that captures their attention. A lot of times it is just stepping out of a car by myself, and people want to know what gadgets I use to drive. (Answer: I don't use gadgets. I drive with one foot on the steering wheel and one on the pedals.) Regardless of what prompts the questions, people will find the courage to very politely ask those questions and have their curiosity satisfied. As the conversation builds, people will take it a step further and want to know how I had gotten to that point in my life. To tell them my life story in a matter of minutes is a difficult proposition, but I do know Who got me there and how He did it. As Paul says in 1 Corinthians 15:10, "by the grace of God I am what I am." Far be it from me to make my life about my own efforts so that I veil the grace of God to the world.

I will never forget one day when I was able to share my testimony with seven different people in the course of about two hours. I had woken up early one morning to, ironically enough, go do sermon prep. I went to a McDonald's that was just a mile from the apartment where my wife and I were living in Greensboro, North Carolina.

When I pulled up I threw my backpack that had my laptop in it on my back and started to walk in to get my breakfast. I walked into the restaurant behind a Greensboro police officer, who was kind enough to hold the door open for me. I walked over to the register, ordered my sandwich and iced coffee, and whipped my debit card out of my shoe to pay.

"Man, you're quick on the draw," the officer said behind me.

"Obviously not as quick as you," I quipped back.

We both had a little laugh, and I went outside and sat at one of the tables to enjoy my fast food feast. I had just finished when I noticed the officer walking over to my table. He sat down across from me, and we stared at each other silently for a couple of seconds. Finally, he said, "Would it be too much trouble if I asked you some questions?"

"As long as it doesn't get me arrested," my smart mouth offered.

He was very interested to know how I did other everyday tasks. He was impressed with how independent I was given my difference. We made mostly small talk for a couple of more minutes until he asked me about how I got to this point.

"How did you keep your disability from crushing you?" he asked with almost a worried look on his face.

"Honestly ... it was a whole lot of grace," I said. That's when I walked through the evidence of God's grace in my life. I talked about how God gave me the perfect parents, the perfect toes, the perfect community of believers, and most importantly—the perfect Savior. Then I walked through the evidence of God's grace in Scripture. I shared John 3, Romans 5, Romans 10, and Ephesians 2.

"I was able to keep this armless mess from crushing me," I told this worried man, "because Jesus gave me a strength and purpose to walk in now, and He gave me the hope of what is to come in eternity. My life became centered on Him and not my wounded, sinful self. He rescued me from my sinful mess and my armless mess."

That's when this man began to cry with me at the picnic table. "Praise God for that, brother. Will you pray for me?" he asked. So here I was at a fast food chain patio, and I was praying with a man I had just met—all of that happened simply because of the way God had made me. Yet God wasn't done with me and this McDonald's.

After I prayed with the officer, he got up to go start his shift on patrol. Once he left, I went back inside to get some hash browns for my still-grumbling belly. I pulled out my debit card and again drew a surprised response from the two guys behind me. They were two landscapers who were grabbing some coffee before they started their workday. But before they enjoyed their coffee, they too wanted to know about my armless situation. I was glad to share with them, much as I had with the officer. After talking with them and encouraging them to pursue Christ more, I took some time to pray over them.

After saying goodbye to those two guys, I scooped my cold hash browns off the counter and went outside to eat them. I chewed through them in no time, but I realized I only had a little bit of ice melt in my cup to wash them down with. I went back inside to get coffee number two for the morning (a coffee appetizer for most pastors!). I got more coffee and headed back outside to start on my sermon prep. When I carry drinks, I definitely draw more stares than other people. For me to carry a drink and walk requires me to hold the cup in the crook of my neck and carefully squeeze it there—much like you would talking on the phone hands-free. This not only makes me an armless guy carrying coffee with his neck; it also makes me look a little hunchbacked as well.

As I made my way outside, a mother and teenage daughter offered to give me a hand. I gratefully accepted, and they walked with me outside to my table. We talked for a few minutes about their plans for the day, and then the conversation shifted to my life with no arms. After I navigated a few of their questions, I took some time to share the hope that I had in Christ. Come to find out that these ladies were fellow believers, and we had a great time encouraging one another. We prayed, hugged, and then said our goodbyes.

I finally sat down to sip on my coffee and start writing out my sermon notes. I had only typed five words when a trio of friends sat down at my table with me. "Are you famous or something?" one of them asked. "We keep seeing all these people talk to you."

I laughed, squirming uncomfortably. "No, I am not famous. This armless thing gets people's attention." We made small talk for a while, and I answered quite a few questions they had about how I could do this or that. I shared with them for a little while more until I asked them a simple question. "I might not be famous, but do you want to hear about someone famous who got me through all this?"

"Of course," a woman in the group replied. I probably didn't tell them about anyone they expected, but I recounted how the King of kings and Lord of lords was with me every step of the way. His fame is bigger than mine will ever be, and I was sure to tell those three friends about Him. I told the woman and her daughter about Him. Those two landscapers. Even Greensboro's finest. That's seven people in all who heard about the legacy of God's grace in my life in just a couple of hours. Not a whole lot of sermon prep happened, but God wrote plenty of lessons on my heart that morning.

The biggest takeaway from that morning was this: the worst and most painful thing that has ever happened to me is honestly the best thing that has ever happened to me. There are so many opportunities and conversations that I have had, solely due to my armlessness. People see my difference and they very quickly perceive all the emotional pain that came with it. Many people can bury their pain or mask it, but my heartache is written all over my two empty sleeves. Those sleeves tell a story without my mouth ever saying a word.

CHAPTER 5

Born to Make Disciples

> "Son, you know you're going to be
> a preacher someday, right?"

People told me this all through my childhood, though few knew that I was not a believer at the time. Once I got saved at the age of fifteen, I still thought the people who said this were completely crazy. I can clearly remember a few weeks after I was saved telling God that there was no way I was going into the ministry. I have since learned that you don't ever tell God the things that you will never do.

Ironically enough, God kept opening doors for me to share my testimony in the months after I was saved. I truly relished the opportunity to share the story of God's grace in my life with other people, but I was honestly horrible at it. First, I am not a natural communicator. I tend to stutter and use filler words repetitively. On stage, I would lose track of what I was saying and stand in awkward silence. Second, the idea of speaking in front of people was entirely intimidating to me. All through my teenage years, every time I had to give my testimony, the night before would be a war of confidence and fear. I would spend much of the night throwing up in the bathroom, and then I'd live off of Pepto-Bismol the next day just so I could survive sharing my testimony.

I was convinced that God had gotten the wrong guy. He kept opening doors to share the gospel, and I happily walked through them. I was just against spending my life in ministry. I had spent the previous seven years planning to go into law (which, oddly enough, involves having to speak in front of a group of people). I did not see that I had the necessary skills to be an effective shepherd in the church, but everyone else saw it. My fear and my flesh kept me from setting my sights on full-time pastoral ministry.

I was a young believer who was hungry to know more of who God was. It was an easy guess to know where I was every Wednesday night, Sunday morning, and Sunday night. It was in that willingness to listen that the Holy Spirit convicted me. One Sunday morning, God sent Clayton King to my church. Clayton shared with our student ministry about some of his recent mission trips. Now, if there is one thing Clayton has going for him, it is that he is a very engaging communicator and storyteller. He had my attention all morning as he recounted his encounters with person after person who was in desperate need of Christ as their Lord.

The morning went from engaging to weighty with each story Clayton shared. I could not shake the conviction that I should be spending my life doing the things that he was talking about. As the morning wrapped up, Clayton challenged us with our own obedience to the Great Commission. "Every believer is charged to go and make disciples," he said. "Is that what your life is about? If it is not making disciples, then something needs to change."

Clayton invited us to accept God's call: I was at the front before the band started playing. I was done running from God. From that point on I was done trying to build my own kingdom. His kingdom and His gospel were going to be my sole aim. I had no idea where to go from there or what a pastor even did, but I was willing to do what it took to become a shepherd within the church.

Word spread among the people of our church about the decision I made that Sunday morning. A number of men approached me to offer encouragement and prayer. My pastors were faithful to challenge me to deepen my faith as I began to pursue ministry.

Discipled in Community

If the first part of my life was centered on determination and self-reliance, it would be fair to characterize this season of my life as one of community and discipleship. I found a clearer sense of my calling through the wise influence of mentors—three men who took me under their wing during my last two years of high school to intentionally disciple and mentor me. My student pastor Dan Bare, apologist Alex McFarland, and local evangelist Dale Elwell poured into me in very unique ways.

Dan helped me to see the value of student ministry. Through my time with him he taught me what it meant to root my entire identity in Christ alone. Living that out as a student pastor meant devoting as much energy to revealing Jesus in a sermon as to showing Jesus to just one person as you sit down for a fast-food breakfast.

God used Alex to help me see the importance of God's Word and to wrap my ministry in it. He had made his entire life about pouring his life into others so that they could perceive the beauty of God and His Word. Alex would come get me from my house once a week, and we'd head off to breakfast at a local restaurant called P & W. It was there that we would talk over difficult passages of Scripture while we ate biscuits and gravy.

Dale was another valuable instrument in God's hands. I traveled with Dale and his family for a few summers while doing ministry alongside them. We would go from eastern North Carolina to Myrtle Beach to deep into the mountains of West Virginia. During these trips Dale would give me opportunities to preach to and counsel students. He would watch at every step along the way and give me crucial feedback on ways that I could improve. Dale also taught me about family and ministry. His entire family—wife and three kids—traveled with him everywhere. I got to see the crucial call for the pastor to shepherd his family while he shepherded the church. To do one at the expense of the other is to completely disregard God's design for the pastor, husband, and father.

My understanding of ministry and my relationship with God were further challenged and deepened at The College at Southeastern, where I attended after high school. Southeastern challenged me on many fronts. I chose to double major in biblical studies and the history of ideas. This course load required nightly fifty- to sixty-page readings of Plato or Aristotle, and I'd have to write weekly five- to ten-page analytical papers on what we were reading. It was overwhelming for a guy like me, an average high school student. I was swimming in the academic deep end while learning to swim at the same time.

My college years were hard from a time-management aspect as well. I had to manage all my reading and writing papers while also trying to generate income. Most college guys can find a job stocking shelves or lifting boxes rather easily, but jobs involving physical labor were out the window for me.

The best route I found was to be a traveling preacher. I did this my entire time in college. This created some scheduling challenges for me. Typically, I'd finish my classes on Thursday night, pack my stuff, and hit the road Friday morning to speak at churches and youth events throughout the Southeast. Many weeks I would finish up late Sunday night and drive through the night to get back to school. I'd catch up on some class assignments and then start back with class on Monday night or early Tuesday morning. It was a grueling pace, but little did I realize how God was preparing me for the relentless pace of full-time ministry.

Southeastern was a valuable resource for me. I had no understanding of what a hermeneutic was or what expositional preaching was until I landed there. I never could have imagined that I would have been accepted like I was there. I was a barefoot, shorts-wearing hippie in a land of suits and button-up shirts, but that did not matter to the professors there. What mattered to them was that I was absorbing the truth of God's Word and then going and telling about it. I am so thankful that God allowed me to soak up so much.

Throughout this season of my life, God was using faithful men to disciple me so that I could know what it looked like to follow Christ and lead others to Him. I was being discipled by these men without ever fully realizing it. By watching the lives of the men whom God kept putting in my life, I was beginning to understand what it looked like to be a faithful follower of Christ.

In 1 Corinthians 10, Paul implores the Corinthian church to have every single corner of one's life aimed at bringing God the glory. At the start of the next chapter Paul says, "Be imitators of me, as I am of Christ" (11:1). Paul had the courage to ask the church to follow his example so that they could know what Christlikeness was. Paul's life was one of the means that God was using to show the Corinthians how to glorify God in all things.

That's exactly what discipleship was meant to be. It is not just a class you take inside the church. For me, it is having a deep, meaningful relationship with a fellow believer so that you can have gospel faithfulness mirrored for you. God put multiple men in my life who very willingly said, "Follow me as I follow Jesus." May we all have the same boldness so that we can sharpen other brothers and sisters in Christ. It was that sort of boldness that helped me deepen my faith and prepare me for the road of ministry ahead.

Stretched by Snowbird

While Southeastern was a great place for me to gain tools for ministry, I knew I needed opportunities to put those tools to use. I had three months every summer to fill with ministry opportunities. I began to scour Google to find the perfect place for me to serve in the summers. Yet every opportunity I found was either not a good fit or I was not qualified for it. I was wrapping up the first semester of my freshman year with no good prospects for the summer. That's when a friend at Southeastern named Becca started to tell me about a camp called Snowbird Wilderness Outfitters.

Now, I already had my preconceived notions about what Christian camps were all about: heavy on fun and light on Jesus. As she talked, Snowbird definitely checked the fun box. Tucked away in the Blue Ridge Mountains of North Carolina, Snowbird specialized in outdoor adventure. Their recreation ranged from whitewater rafting to rappelling to caving and backpacking.

What Becca said next about the camp sold me. She said Snowbird was dedicated to the gospel. Every square inch of how they operated was aimed at proclaiming God's Word to students and the nations. Their schedule alone showed where their priorities were: two worship sessions a day, one breakout session a day, a leader's breakout session every morning, and a student-to-staff ratio of three-to-one to promote meaningful conversations about the students' faith. That night, I went to their website and printed out their application. I spent the next week filling out their

nine-page theological questionnaire. It wasn't until I finished the application that I realized I was three weeks late.
I submitted it anyway and prayed for some grace.

A couple of weeks later I got a call from a weird area code.
"Hey," the voice on the other end boomed. "Is this Daniel?"

"Yes, sir."

"You really don't have arms?"

"Uhhh ... no, sir, I don't."

"Okay. You're hired."

"Wait. What?"

That was my introduction to Brody Holloway, director
of Snowbird Wilderness Outfitters. He said I had missed
the deadline for applying, but once they had read my testimony about not having arms, they were set on bringing
me on staff. For them, the opportunity of having an armless
guy on staff was too good to pass up. We were both excited
at the promise of being able to partner in ministry.

This partnership was not without its steep learning
curve. Outdoor adventure camps and armless people are
not exactly a match made in heaven. Many aspects of outdoor adventure require arms, and there is no matter of
being able to adapt around it. One of the things we had to
work around was that every staff member would guide a
raft down the Nantahala River on every Thursday during
camp. It is impossible for an armless guy to hold a paddle
and guide a raft. Our very first week of staff training was
dedicated to training on guiding on the river, so the guys
at Snowbird had to think of something for me to do while
everyone else was on the river.

Their first thought was to have me do odd jobs around camp … like whacking weed around our entire pasture fence. I can use a Weedwhacker with a degree of success, but it means that I must sit down on the ground to hold it with both feet and then scoot on my rear end to keep moving along. The only down side is that I get covered in grass from about the chin on down, but I gladly accepted the opportunity to show the Snowbird staff that this arm-less experiment could work.

Off I went to mow down a bunch of weeds. It was a few hours into my work that I think that Brody had visions of me losing what two limbs I had left in a horrific Weed-whacking accident. When I finished the job after a few hours, I hopped back into the truck to find that I had three voicemails from Brody—all three saying he hoped that I had not actually gone on with the plan. When I got back to camp, he admitted that he had forgotten I didn't have arms, which I think is one of the greatest compliments someone can give me.

I could tell probably a hundred other funny stories from camp. The time I wiped out an entire team of high school boys in paintball. The time a leader cried because an arm-less person got in a van to drive her and some students to a hiking trip. The time I dressed up as an armless hot dog luchador for a skit. Those funny memories are ones that I think I'll hold onto for the rest of my life, but that is not my takeaway from my four summers there. The gospel is the legacy of Snowbird. The gospel in the lives of students. It matters in the preaching. It matters in the music. It matters in the one-on-one conversations. It matters in every single corner of a ministry. That has followed me at every ministry stop along the way since my time in the North Carolina mountains.

Snowbird also helped me fall in love with student ministry. To watch young men and women move along the process of sanctification is a beautiful thing to watch. I wanted to be a part of a ministry that walks with students from unbeliever to convert to passionate newbie to committed disciple and beyond. I now can say I have seen eleven years as a student pastor, and I pray I get to see eleven more.

Sure, there are plenty of times when I think my body can't hold up to sleeping on a foam mattress for six days at camp. There are the times I talk about the music I used to listen to on cassette and my middle schoolers look at me like I grew arms. I hope I don't grow too old to serve students because I can't think of another thing I'd rather do than to invest in and disciple future doctors, lawyers, engineers, moms, dads, pastors, or missionaries. It is incredible that I get to invest in these students who are simultaneously the church of today and the church of tomorrow.

I truly love my job, even with all the difficulties that come with being a pastor. I would not trade this for anything else in the world. The call to make disciples day in and day out is an amazing opportunity. There are costs that you must count much in the same way that you must count the cost of being a disciple.

I know there are some of you who are reading this and praying about going into full-time ministry. If that is you, I want you to know that ministry is hard. The hours are long and irregular. Your family will bear the burden of the constant stress of the job. You will constantly see people at their worst. There will be seasons that you will want to quit and get a different job. You will have days that will make you wonder why God called you in the first place.

That's when God reminds you why He called you. It is because your life is about His kingdom and not yours. It is because He is going to get all the glory and you are set to get none of it. It is because He wants to set you apart and not to just set you up for earthly success. It is because it is about His claim on your life and not your comfort.

As a matter of fact, that call is to come and die. Die to yourself, die to your wants, and die to this world. Our aim is to make His name great among all peoples and nations, but we have the honor of starting to make His name great among all people. Whether you are called to full-time ministry or not, every believer is called to make disciples. Even if that means pouring your life into one or two believers while also working your nine to five, the cost of making disciples is well worth it.

No Excuses

I sometimes thought the cost of making disciples was too great for me to handle. It is funny to think that I built my independence on not quitting or giving in to excuses, but I wavered the moment that stepping into ministry became an option. I can clearly remember my prayer life being filled with a whole lot of, "But, God—"

> But, God—I am a horrible speaker.
> But, God—I am an introvert.

> But, God—I have no idea how to do this.
> But, God—people aren't going to see past this
>   armless thing.

I was the young Christian who had staked my young faith on Philippians 4:13. I was living like God could help me overcome anything ... except my fear of ministry. I was buying the lie heard in the garden, "Did God really say?" That was the only question that the snake offered Eve to get her to fling herself into disobedience. It was the same lie that I was diving into wholeheartedly because it was the easy thing to do. I didn't want to walk another hard road. I had been down so many trying to learn to eat, write, and dress myself. I was happy to not fight this battle, until God took me across Jeremiah 1:

Now the word of the Lord came to me, saying,

"Before I formed you in the womb I knew you,
    and before you were born I consecrated you;
I appointed you a prophet to the nations."

Then I said, "Ah, Lord God! Behold, I do not know how to speak, for I am only a youth." But the Lord said to me,

"Do not say, 'I am only a youth';
    for to all to whom I send you, you shall go,
    and whatever I command you, you shall speak.
Do not be afraid of them, for I am with you
        to deliver you,
    declares the Lord." (Jeremiah 1:4–8)

God has a way of stopping excuse-filled hearts with His very words. Jeremiah wanted to hold up his age and lack of wisdom as evidence for his uselessness in ministry. God had only to say that age is just a number and Jeremiah's words would be the very words of the Lord. The same words that formed the earth. The same words that always accomplish their purpose. The same words that are sharper than any double-edged sword. God had made Jeremiah for this, equipped him for this, and was there to walk with him through it all.

Excuses extinguished.

In digging into the life of Jeremiah even further, you see how he earns the label of "weeping prophet." His message centered on the sinfulness of Israel and their need to turn back to the Lord. He gets persecuted by his own family, and, because Israel ignores the words of the Lord, Jeremiah suffers through the destruction of Jerusalem. This suffering prophet who told of the suffering of sin to come must suffer through his obedience to what the Lord sent him to do.

Excuses are meaningless to the God who made all things.

Suffering is the brand of the believer. That truth left me in convicted silence as I sat in front of God's legacy in the life of Jeremiah. I had been told lies from the enemy and had bought them. I saw an easy road, and I was happy to take it. But what in the life of Christ was built of excuses or ease? He didn't step off that cross when the very people He was dying for spat on Him. He didn't bail when He was born in a barn and not a palace. The life of my Lord was absent of ease and excuse. In fact, the life of Christ shows a redemption bought willingly in His own blood.

So why do I so easily divorce the life of the disciple from the example of the Savior? Why do I expect comfort when my Lord had anything but that? Why do I whine and complain when the perfect Lamb who stepped down from the right hand of the Father was silent before His shearers?

The cost of discipleship is a hard reality for all of us to count. It is a reality that makes the Great Commission a choice between comfort or obedience. Either we go and make disciples, or we disobey. The Great Commission is not a mission statement for pastors; it is marching orders for the church. Either we buy excuses to justify our disobedience or we rest in grace so that we may speak of grace. The choice is ours.

Talk about a hard reality to swallow. Equally, what a hard reality that our Savior conquered sin and death so that we can have eternal life. It is in that beauty that we rest in and can have the courage to stand. It is that gospel beauty that the believer can abide in and tell of. It is when we savor the beauty of Christ that we want to share that sort of sweetness with the world. That's why in Acts 20:24 Paul can boldly say: "But I do not account my life of any value nor as precious to myself, if only I may finish my course and the ministry that I received from the Lord Jesus, to testify to the gospel of the grace of God."

Why is Paul able to stare at life itself and choose Christ over comfort? Because grace is better than comfort. Gospel words are better than excuse-encrusted silence. Christ gave us a calling that sets captives free and calls people from death to life. The church cannot be silent about that. There is too much at stake for a lost and dying world for disciples to accept the lie heard in the garden. Some of us may never step on the mission field or walk into a pulpit, and that is perfectly fine. We all accept the call to make disciples the moment we call on Jesus as Lord.

The question is not if we're called to make disciples; the question is a question of when and where.

CHAPTER 6

Born to Love and Be Loved

"Will you marry me?"

Those were words I thought I would never be able to utter for a myriad of reasons. First, I struggled daily to see the beauty of my exterior. How would a woman be able to see it? Second is that no one wants to live in a fish bowl, which is what you would get by committing to spend a life with me. No trip to the store and no romantic date would be complete without several stares. Lastly comes the difficult task of being a pastor's wife. That's a role that comes with difficult and unspoken expectations. It is a sort of fish bowl that goes even deeper than just being an armless man's wife. You are signing up to be an armless pastor's wife. Marrying me came with a warning label.

I had plenty of reasons to feel I wasn't marriage material. I dated a few girls in high school, but we never got serious enough to talk marriage. I was fine with that. By my sophomore year of college, I was beginning to accept singleness as a possible future for me. I had thought I would finish out college working at Snowbird in the summers and then settle into full-time camp ministry with those guys at camp. I had my plan all figured out.

That is, until *she* walked into Snowbird. It was my second year at camp, and I had just arrived for staff training. I was standing with some of the guys I had worked with the year before, and we were catching up with everything that had happened in the last nine months. And that is when it happened. She walked by. My brain stopped working. She looked like a hippie, her curly blonde hair tucked behind a rolled-up bandana. She was tall and had a killer smile. I had to get to know this girl.

Earlier, my college roommate, Tyler, had told me I should be on the lookout for a girl named Heather. Tyler said they had been friends for years. He described her as an artsy, free-spirited girl who loved the outdoors. She sounded like someone I wanted to get to know, but I had no idea who she was beyond a few adjectives.

Was this blonde beauty the same girl whom Tyler had told me about? I had no clue, but I thought I'd approach her and introduce myself.

"Hey, my name is Daniel."

"I'm Heather."

"Heather Crews?"

"Yeah. How'd you know?"

"Tyler told me about you."

"Okay. Cool."

That was it. That was just about as far as our conversation stretched. People talk about love at first sight and fireworks when they first met, but ours was a three-minute conversation full of awkward silence. Not exactly an inter-action that spawns any sort of hope of a friendship, much less a romance. It is not like romantic moments were in our future in the first place—dating was not allowed among staff at camp. You were there to make much of Jesus, not to make much of the person whom you happen to work with.

Even so, we would cross paths at camp a good bit. We often worked the same activity, and sometimes we would sit together for a quick meal in the cafeteria before heading off to the next thing that there was for us to do. We spent three months together at camp, sporadically spending time around each other. We had begun to kindle a friendship. Heather returned to Western Carolina University, and I went back to The College of Southeastern, placing us about 300 miles away from each other. To me, it seemed like this relationship was doomed to fizzle.

The only upside was that Heather's home was in Raleigh, North Carolina, which was about fifteen minutes from my school's campus. Anytime she came back home, she'd invite me over for dinner with her family. That was an invitation I would gladly accept. My school didn't have any dining options on campus. I was surviving on mac and cheese and Dinty Moore microwavable meals. Basically, I was in des-perate need of tasty food. Add in the fact that I was trying to get to know Heather better, and you better believe that I showed up whenever she invited.

This went on every other weekend for about two months. We started to talk on the phone. We laughed, cried, and prayed over the phone. Our relationship was beginning to build toward more than just friendship, which pushed me deep into prayer and soul-searching. I did not want to string Heather along in a dead-end relationship if I thought she wasn't the woman I was going to marry. If she was *the one* I wanted to be sure before I told her.

Little did I know that on the other side of North Carolina, Heather was asking her best friend to pray about our relationship. Heather's prayer was that we would decide what our relationship was—friendship or something more—and that I would take the leadership in this. We were both seeking God's guidance with how this relationship needed to go forward. After weeks in prayer and some fasting, I had my answer: Heather was the woman I was going to marry.

Now the question was, *Did she think the same thing?* Up until this point, we had never been on a date together and never talked about dating or marriage. I had no idea how she would react to my telling her that I thought she was the one. I was truly taking a shot in the dark, but I was going to take the chance on it.

Heather came home one weekend in October 2005 to take her little brother Aaron to the state fair in Raleigh. Being a country boy, I loved to eat every single unhealthy food option that fairs have to offer, so I asked to tag along. We spent all day at the fair and had a blast. We ate funnel cake, looked at the farm animals, and soaked in everything the fair had to offer. All the while, Heather was funny, caring, and free-spirited. I was getting a small glimpse of what life with her would be like, and I was sold. I decided I was going to propose to Heather … that night.

I didn't have a ring for her, but that didn't matter much to me. I knew the time was right. We drove back to her parents' house to drop her brother off, and then Heather drove me back to my duplex at college.

When we pulled up to my place, I asked if she wanted to talk inside for a little bit, and she gladly accepted. We made small talk for a while in my ratty little duplex. Then, I slowly started to move the conversation to our relationship. I did not want to come completely out of the blue with a proposal. I at least wanted to make sure she saw something more than just a friendship. But the more we talked, the more my fears were staved off. It was now or never.

Finally, I said the words that I had prayed over for weeks on end and now waited with racing heart to hear her response: "Will you marry me?"

She did not even hesitate. "Yes. Yes, I'll marry you."

We both laughed, cried, and hugged for quite a while after our ringless proposal. Once the reality of what we had just committed to set in, I knew I needed to go a step further. I went into the kitchen and got a bowl of water and a dish towel. I came back into the living room with the towel over my shoulder and bowl in my toes. I sat down in front of my fiancée to wash her feet and pray for her.

I prayed over her life and pursuit of Christ. I prayed for our marriage to come. I prayed over the life of ministry that we would embark on together. I prayed for the kids that we would one day have. I prayed that I would be vigilant to lead her, love her, fight for her, and serve her.

With everything that we would certainly face as a married couple in ministry, I knew we absolutely had to begin our marriage relationship with Christ as the foundation. We were certain to come against unrelenting trials and attacks from the enemy, but we were going to anchor ourselves, and our marriage, to the One who stitched the world together and who was about to stitch our two lives into one.

We were married only nine months later, on July 29, 2006. We planned the wedding relatively easily. We arranged the ceremony and reception. We put a bridal party together quickly. We had a honeymoon destination worked out. But the one thing we struggled with was: where do you put a wedding ring on an armless man? We had given thought to a toe ring, but for as much as I am barefoot, a toe ring would have been impractical—it would have taken a lot of wear and tear. We considered putting a ring on a necklace, but I didn't like the idea of covering it up under my shirts.

That was when my ever-creative wife came up with the idea to put a ring in the top portion of cartilage in my left ear. It was the perfect idea. It made my wedding ring clearly visible, and it wouldn't hamper my day-to-day life. So, on that Saturday in July, we said our "I do's," I slipped her ring on her hand with my toes, and she put the ring in my ear. Before God we pledged to pursue one another as we pursued Him.

A True Helpmate

I am so thankful our commitment to Him was the bedrock of our relationship because we were in for all kinds of trials in our young marriage.

As soon as we got back from our honeymoon, I started a job as an associate youth pastor at my home church,

Pleasant Garden Baptist Church. Heather started at the University of North Carolina at Greensboro pursuing a degree in fine art and design. With a one-income family (a part-time ministry income at that), we were flat broke. We lived in a 650-square-foot apartment on the south side of Greensboro. We had enough money in our budget to take one date night out a month … to Wendy's. Financial stress was a burden in our young marriage.

Two weeks after we had embarked on this new life as a married ministry couple, my dad called me and asked me to meet him at a local park to walk and talk. It was on this walk he told me he had been diagnosed with stage three small cell lung cancer. The doctors had told him that he wouldn't live past Christmas. It was September.

I was devastated and overwhelmed. I felt like I could barely provide for my wife. I was about to lose my lifelong advocate and dad. It was as if my entire world was spinning out of control. Through all of this, Heather stood right beside me. We would weep together and pray together. We would recount God's promises together. We would cling to the evidence of God's grace and power in Scripture, especially in the life of Abraham. He was a man whom God had called to an unseen land and had been promised descendants he did not yet have. Throughout all that, Abraham trusted. Abraham obeyed. Abraham went.

So we trusted. We obeyed to the best of our abilities. We went where God called us. We still had times of trial and fear early in our marriage, but God sustained us. He found a way to provide for us with our meager budget. He healed my dad, who, as of 2017, is still alive ten years after a grave diagnosis. God sustained both of us and provided me with the perfect helpmate through it all.

"Helpmate" is exactly what describes my wife. She is the complement to me in so many ways and balances me out in the things that I struggle with. I am a disorganized, abstract thinker who is often spur-of-the-moment. Heather is carefully organized with an artistic flair and makes plans to meet her goals. God knew what He was doing when He made our two lives become one. She was put into my life to balance me out, to serve alongside me, and to love me.

God's Glory in Marriage

That is the love I was certain that I would never know when I was single. I was convinced I was going to be alone for the span of my life. I felt like Adam in Genesis 2, alone with an intimidating call in front of me. Yet God saw fit in His grace that I should not be alone, and he sent Heather my way. He sent me my best friend, my partner in ministry, and the love of my life.

She has embraced so much of the difficult life that has been placed in front of us. Many pastors' wives struggle with many of the unseen and untold pressures that come with your husband's being in full-time ministry. The only married life that Heather has known is as a pastor's wife, and it is a life she has embraced. In my ten years in student ministry, she has been an active part of the day-to-day life of the ministry. She goes on many of our mission trips and camps. She carves out time in her afternoon to sit down and counsel teenage girls who are struggling through hurt and fear. She actively disciples the girls of our student ministry so that they can truly taste and see that the Lord is good.

She has worked her tail off in the ten years we've been married. Early on in our marriage when I was only part-time at my church, Heather chose to take on a part-time job to help make ends meet while she was still a full-time college student and wife. It just so happens that the only part-time job this pastor's wife could find was at Victoria's Secret. While some people may have looked negatively at a pastor's wife working at a lingerie store, Heather jumped at the chance. This was her opportunity to serve our family in our need. She did it without complaint, much like she did at her other jobs through our married life. She worked in multiple schools as a teacher's assistant in a class for kids with behavioral and emotional disorders. Where many people saw broken kids beyond repair, Heather saw a chance to show kids the love of Christ that they desperately needed.

All the while, as she served as pastor's wife and faithful employee, her heart longed for the day that she could be a mom. After five years of marriage, God allowed us to conceive our first child, a son named Teague, in 2010. However, bringing Teague into the world was not without its own trial. It wasn't long into Heather's pregnancy that her doctors started to notice something out of the ordinary. Tests revealed that the stress of pregnancy was fueling the growth of a benign tumor on Heather's uterus. Doctors would have been content to leave the tumor until after Teague's birth, but its growth rate was astronomical.

By seventeen weeks into Heather's pregnancy, the tumor was the size of a beach ball. It had to come out.

Again, fear flooded our hearts. The surgery posed a risk to both Heather and our unborn son. The most fear-inducing aspect was that the stress of the surgery could send Heather into labor, and there was no chance for our son to survive at seventeen weeks. We were both terrified and broken. I remember those days before the surgery were filled with prayer and Scripture. It was through the heartache mixed with prayer that we came to the place of trust. God had shown Himself incredibly faithful through both of our lives and through our marriage. He had never abandoned us or left us without hope. Our minds would go to one of Heather's favorite verses, Romans 11:36: "For from him and through him and to him are all things. To him be glory forever. Amen."

God had ransomed us both and called us a son and a daughter. God had brought us together as husband and wife. God was intricately weaving our son together in Heather's womb. He had brought us through so much, and through it all He had shown Himself faithful and glorious. At the end of this surgery, He would still be faithful and glorious—regardless of the outcome.

The doctors wheeled Heather back to surgery after we had prayed together. As she went under the knife to remove this tumor, I had to battle through waves of fear and doubt. I sat in the waiting room having my heart flip back and forth between the pictures of God's faithfulness and the fear of possibly losing the two people whom I loved the most in this world. I clung to Him in the middle of that cold waiting room, not knowing if I would ever cling to my wife ever again, but God graciously carried my wife through the surgery.

Flash forward to April 21, 2012: we met our newborn son for the first time. As we celebrated the grace of God giving us our son Teague, our hearts were almost bursting with thanks. Teague was the gift that a faithful and glorious God had given us. Yet we both knew that God would still be faithful and glorious if we had lost our son on that operating table those weeks before. God had graciously carried us through our young marriage, and He would continue to do so, even if we had lost our son. I know it is easy for us to say on this side of His gracious gift of our son, but our hearts were prepared for the worst. We did not know how He would get us through, but we knew He would. Just like my parents knew God would get them through the birth of their armless son. God is faithful and glorious—even in my pain and doubt. That is what we were fixing our hearts to.

The one thing I love about my wife the most is that God's glory is at the center of everything she does. She stays at home with our two kids—Teague and our daughter, Elliott. She views this as her ministry and as a way to show the gospel to our two kids. By loving them and serving them, it is her prayer that our kids can clearly see God's love in her and they can savor how amazing He is. As she loves our kids, she is also an entrepreneur who runs her own calligraphy business called Heather's Letters. Even in her business, it is her prayer that through her artistic gifts people can get a small glimpse of the beauty of who God is.

Her heart to love, serve, and glorify the Father is beautiful. There are many days when her passion for God's glory reminds me to show Him to everyone I encounter. Our simple prayer is that in our lives and in our marriage, people may get a small taste of the sweetness of who God is, that they may in turn make their lives about His glory.

CHAPTER 7

Love Like the Father

"What if the baby doesn't have arms?"

As we prepared to have our first baby, I didn't have many fears about being a new dad. Still, I was a little uncertain of how to hold a baby when you don't have any hands. I knew I would have to be creative in fastening a diaper without the benefit of thumbs. I knew playing a game of catch in the backyard would be a difficult proposition. That was the word I kept preparing myself with: difficult. These things were going to be hard and require some adjustment on my part, but I knew I could do it.

Early in our marriage I was truly excited to be a dad one day, but there was one fear in my heart that I could not possibly shake free until I saw the first ultrasound: what if my child is born without arms?

The question did not bother me from a purely physical standpoint. Honestly, who better to raise an armless baby than an armless daddy? I'd be the perfect person to show baby Ritchie the ropes of life without arms. It was the emotional burden that comes with being born without arms that really troubled me. I knew the weight that came with being different from everyone else and not having any way to hide it. I knew the frustration that came with trying to make your feet and legs do things that were meant for hands and arms. I knew how harsh someone's careless insults can cut through the fabric of a person's identity. There wasn't an ounce of myself that wanted that for my kid.

Once we found out we were expecting our first child, I peppered our OB/GYN with questions about whether my armless condition could be passed down genetically. Our doctor could not give us a straight answer. I waited impatiently for our very first ultrasound appointment. As we got Heather prepped for the ultrasound, I just prayed—mostly that God would settle my fearful heart. I prayed that I would be joyful in whatever I was about to see. I rested in the truth that a child with arms or no arms was still my child and that was enough.

The moment the ultrasound screen flashed on, my eyes instantly began to scan back and forth. It took a second for my eyes to adjust to the images of our baby. As my eyes begin to settle, I didn't need to ask the ultrasound technician anything. Right in the middle of the screen was our son, sucking on his thumb. Our little boy had two arms and ten fingers.

With the fear of passing along my armlessness relieved and Heather's scary surgery out of the way, I was beyond ready to be a daddy. I had daydreams of getting on the floor and wrestling my son. I looked forward to fall afternoons of running around and playing football. As dreams began to be a reality, we started to prep for Teague to come into our family. We bought diapers, baby clothes, and toys. We bought a crib, and I put it together with my toes. We got every bit of his nursery set up to be filled with laughs and cries very soon.

As the delivery date came closer, we packed our overnight bags for the hospital. We had it all planned out. Heather had decided to stop working two weeks before her due date so that we had plenty of time to finish all the last-minute prep for our son to arrive. We celebrated Heather's last day of work and headed to my last youth ministry event before our son's due date: a Thirty-Hour Famine Lock-In. Students fast for thirty hours while raising money to stop malnutrition and hunger across the globe. At the end of the fast, the students come together to talk through global missions, break the fast, and celebrate what God had done.

We got to church at 7:00 p.m. to spend time in worship and have some fun. By midnight, my eight-and-a-half-month-pregnant wife was spent. She headed back home to get some well-deserved sleep. Two hours later my cell phone rang. "Your son is on the way!" she said. I hadn't slept or eaten in eighteen hours, but I could not have been more ready or excited. I was ready to meet our son.

We sped to the hospital with joy in our hearts. After eighteen-and-a-half hours of labor, we welcomed Teague into the world. There are so many aspects of that moment that I will never forget. There are so many images from that day that are locked into my brain. They all fill my heart with such joy. Yet the feelings of that day are something that I will never forget. They are all feelings that I can barely even put into words.

Loving the Mess of Life

I knew that being a father would be an experience unlike any other—but I had no idea how many things I would learn about myself and God until the moment I first met Teague. My sense of love for Teague in that moment was completely overwhelming. Love is such a funny emotion. It is so remarkably deep and complex, but we think we understand it. I remember being a teenager and thinking that there was no way I could love something as much as I loved the Carolina Panthers. Well, that seems incredibly stupid now. When Heather and I got engaged I thought I truly understood love. I mean, I was committing my life to someone else. It doesn't get much more loving than that, right? When Heather and I got married my perspective deepened even further. Two lives became one. I set my heart to love her before I loved myself. I pursued and protected her at all costs. Then Teague came along, and my understanding deepened even more.

Here was this little boy whom my wife was holding whom I had just physically met—but I loved him more than my own life. He had literally done nothing but cry in his first few minutes of life, and I could not be prouder of him. A fatherly affection was kindled inside me that I didn't expect. I loved Teague in a way that I had never loved anyone else before. It wasn't as if I hadn't understand true love before that moment, but the experiences of my life were all helping to show the mystery of the gospel and God's love for me.

In marrying Heather, I had the opportunity to live out the beauty of Ephesians 5 with regard to Christ and the church. I was to live out Ephesians 5:25—"Husbands, love your wives, as Christ loved the church and gave himself up for her"—by giving up my very life as Christ did for the church. I was to bathe our marriage in the Word just like we see in verse 26. I saw the challenge of verse 29 as I needed to seek daily to nourish and cherish my bride. My love for my bride was helping me to understand Christ's love for His bride, the church.

Then our son Teague came on the scene, followed by our gorgeous daughter, Elliott, a few years later. Both of my kids allowed me to be a dad—and, in turn, to love them as their dad. There was now this tangible experience of *my* love as a father that allowed me to understand the love of my Heavenly Father. It is an affection that comes without condition or excuse. It is a love that shows itself in laughter and a love that shows itself in discipline. It is a love that can even be messy at times, but that is what comes with the territory of being a parent.

Kids just make a mess of things sometimes. As of this writing, my son is five years old and can function like a small tornado. He plays with multiple toys at the same time, and then he will suddenly move on to playing with a couple of different toys. He goes through this process over and over until the toy box is emptied and the room looks like it had a hand grenade dropped into it.

So there is this messy aspect of who Teague is, but there is also something else to know about Teague: he's a big boy. For a long time he was just a tall, chunky baby—ninetieth percentile in height and ninetieth percentile in weight. If things go how the doctors predict, our boy will grow to be six foot four one day. He's my big boy. My big, messy little boy. That is the way he has been for the first five years of his life, and I see no signs of that stopping anytime soon.

Teague and I have always had a tight bond. We have always said that he is full of "boy joy"—basically, he likes to do anything boyish and has a blast doing those things. A couple of years ago, Heather left me with our big bunch of boy joy so she could get some time for herself. That afternoon we did every single car-related thing that you could possibly do with a two-year-old boy. We took Hot Wheel cars and raced them all through the house. When that got boring, we raced the cars until they invariably crashed into each other. When that got boring, we built a wall out of blocks and crashed the cars into that.

Finally, when the cars had run their course we did what most boys like to do: we wrestled. It was in between all the wrestling and tickling that I got a whiff of something stinky. Every parent knows that dreaded dirty-diaper smell, and that is exactly what I was smelling. So of course, I grabbed Teague so that we could get this stinky diaper changed. I rolled out the diaper-changing blanket on the floor. I then picked up a clean diaper and the box of wipes so we could get back to having man time.

It was only once I had busted open Teague's diaper that I realized how stinky and messy it really was. Let's just say I was equal parts impressed and scared. Once I surveyed the landscape of what I needed to do, I grasped a baby wipe between my toes. As I moved both feet in so I could do what I needed to do, my little man unleashed the most body-contorting sneeze I have ever heard a toddler unleash.

To my horror, this powerful baby burst caused my son's butt cheeks to smack the bottom of my feet, covering them in baby poop. I sat on the floor in partial shock, and my son lay there in silent pride of his newfound superpower. I realized there was no way I could get him cleaned up without spreading the mess everywhere.

To top everything else off, I was holding the last wipe from the box in my toes, which were now completely messed up. My only way to remedy the situation was going to be scoot on my butt from the living room to the kitchen so that I could hop up on the counter and wash my feet. I nudged Teague a toy, pleaded with him to stay on the blanket while I was gone, and then started the long scoot from the living room to the kitchen. As I inched my way across the bottom floor of our townhome, I had horrific visions of Teague hopping off that blanket and painting our living room with his little tush.

I managed to get to the sink in the kitchen, hopped up on the counter, and washed my feet in the sink as fast as I possibly could. I hopped off the counter and sprinted into the living room, only to find Teague ... lying exactly where I left him. He hadn't moved a muscle. I walked to the other side of the living room to grab more wipes and came back to get Teague all cleaned up. Once I got a new diaper on him, I scooped him up with my legs and gave him a big hug. All I could do was squeeze him and laugh. My big, messy son was being just that—my big, messy son. Our little diaper mishap made him no less my son than when we were crashing cars. He was still my boy; how could I not love him?

Learning the Father's Love

My love for my children is strong, but I know that it is just a glimpse of what the Father's love is for me. It is a lesson I think many of us grasp to one degree or another, but is it a reality I dwell in? When was the last time I sat down and just soaked in the fact that the Creator of the universe loves me? My mind instantly takes me to the words of Jesus in John 15:9–13:

> As the Father has loved me, so have I loved you. Abide in my love. If you keep my commandments, you will abide in my love, just as I have kept my Father's commandments and abide in his love. These things I have spoken to you, that my joy may be in you, and that your joy may be full. "This is my commandment, that you love one another as I have loved you. Greater love has no one than this, that someone lay down his life for his friends."

This passage includes almost too many nuggets of truth. A few things to glean from John 15: first, Jesus loved His disciples in the same way the Heavenly Father loved Him. The love of the world that Jesus explained to the self-righteous Nicodemus is graciously given and not earned. The love Christ had for the sinful Samaritan woman is a love that the Father has for a lost and dying world. The love Jesus showed His broke, ragtag bunch of disciples shows a love that disregards socioeconomic background. The love of the Father, as seen in the ministry of Jesus, is a love that spills over any sort of human label.

Second is the call for us to abide in His love. It is the call to sit down in, live in, and trust in the love that Jesus has for us. The call to abide spans past a plain knowledge of the fact that Jesus loves me. It is a life-altering bedding down in the fact that my God loves me. Romans 8:31–39 goes a long way to describe the promise of this love:

> What then shall we say to these things? If God is for us, who can be against us? He who did not spare his own Son but gave him up for us all, how will he not also with him graciously give us all things? Who shall bring any charge against God's elect? It is God who justifies. Who is to condemn? Christ Jesus is the one who died—more than that, who was raised—who is at the right hand of God, who indeed is interceding for us. Who shall separate us from the love of Christ? Shall tribulation, or distress, or persecution, or famine, or nakedness, or danger, or sword? As it is written,
>
>> "For your sake we are being killed all the day long;
>> we are regarded as sheep to be slaughtered."
>
> No, in all these things we are more than conquerors through him who loved us. For I am sure that neither death nor life, nor angels nor rulers, nor things present nor things to come, nor powers, nor height nor depth, nor anything else in all creation, will be able to separate us from the love of God in Christ Jesus our Lord.

No circumstance, person, or power is going to rip us away from God's love for us. Imagine how life-changing it is for us to not simply know that but to live in that promise daily. In our abiding there is an element of personal holiness—keeping the commandments that He has set in front of us. It is by abiding in His love that He changes us, and it is by abiding in His love in keeping His commandments that we display that love in this broken world.

Third is the depth of the love that Christ shows in the gospel. John 15:13 reminds us that there is no greater love that someone can show than to lay down his life for the people he loves. Yet Jesus takes the love of God a step further by dying for the people who hated Him. Romans 5:10 paints the picture of Christ loving us as enemies—"For if while we were enemies we were reconciled to God by the death of his Son, much more, now that we are reconciled, shall we be saved by his life." This incredible verse points us to the fact that Jesus went to the cross to save those who are lost in sin and those who have turned their backs on Him. We were all His enemies, and Jesus went to the cross so that He could be the first born of many brothers. The love displayed in the cross stretches deeper than any conceivable earthly love.

It is that gospel love that I want to sow into my kids' hearts. That is the sort of sharing the gospel that I love more than anything in the world. I have preached in other countries and in front of large crowds, but I can't think of anything I would rather do than to sit with my son and my daughter and to read to them something like their *Jesus Storybook Bible* or *The Biggest Story*. Neither one of my kids is old enough to grasp what it is to make Jesus their Lord, but there is nothing that makes me well up with pride more than when I can see my son beginning to talk through biblical principles with his friends or with a passerby.

And when we sow these small seeds of the gospel, sometimes the victories are small but carry great joy. It is a joy to see these biblical truths beginning to lodge themselves in my son's heart. At the age of five, my son is just beginning to understand that his daddy is different than everyone else. Other kids Teague's age will often ask, "Why does your dad eat with his feet?" or "Why doesn't your dad have any arms?" Those are really hard questions for a preschooler to tackle, and understandably he wouldn't quite know how to respond to those questions. But one day a few months ago, my son blew me away when someone asked Teague why I didn't have any arms. He replied, "Well, that is the way Jesus made him."

Talk about a proud-dad moment. My kid was starting to grasp some of the most basic truths about God fearfully crafting each one of us. While basking in the joy of being a daddy, I think of the rejoicing of the Father when one of His lost sheep turns to Him. "Just so, I tell you, there is joy before the angels of God over one sinner who repents" (Luke 15:10). This passage tells us that joy breaks out in heaven when a sinner repents and rests in Christ. The joy that the Father will have when my own son lays His life at the feet of the Father will trump my own joy over Teague's trusting in Christ. It is that picture of my son grasping gospel reality after gospel reality that warms my heart, but it is the thought of his eternal hope and purpose resting in Christ that drives me.

My wife and I are also blessed to be able to sow the seeds of the gospel into the heart of our two-year-old girl named Elliott. She is a little girl who is fierce, fun, strong willed, and knows what she wants. Yet this strong girl has a reserved and watchful side to her that is precious to watch. Anytime she meets someone for the first time, she keenly observes a person's demeanor to see if she wants to go any further in opening herself up to him or her.

It is this watchfulness that has also made our father/ daughter relationship so unique. Early on in her life, probably when she was a year old, she realized I could not pick her up like her mom can with her arms. But it was through wrestling and playing with me that she realized I could pick her up in another way. She figured out that if I squatted down, she could walk up behind me, wrap her arms around my neck, and then she would hold on tight. Even to this day that is the way that I carry her around—as my little baby backpack. It is this sort of watchfulness that is the reminder that our children are always watching and learning. So what are we teaching our kids?

For all of us dads, our heart should be to shepherd our families in view of who God is. Every step of our lives must hinge on the fact that it is the responsibility of the family as well as the church to make disciples of our kids. The weight of Deuteronomy 6 should follow us every step we take as husbands and dads. We are called to teach our kids the commands of God whether we are in our home or we are out and about. The most loving thing that any of us will do as dads is to point our kids to the love and glory of the Father. The One from whom and through whom and for whom are all things.

The burden of discipleship falls on dads first ... and then the church. Can that be said of our families? Am I personally investing in the spiritual maturity of my child, or am I solely depending on the church to disciple my kid?

If you're sitting here feeling slightly convicted over not discipling your own kid, you are not alone. The vast majority of student ministries, including ones I lead for a time, operate as if discipleship could only occur in a Sunday school class or a small group on campus at a church. Yet, over the last few years, student ministries have begun to realize that disciples cannot be made in an investment of one hour a week. Disciples are made over time through deep relational and spiritual investment. Who better to disciple a kid than the people who are in chief authority and closest proximity to a kid? The parents.

There is no need to be intimidated at the prospect of discipling your child. You don't need to take a class or receive a certificate; you just need to start. Start by reading Scripture with your kids for a few minutes a day. Spend time in prayer with your kids. Take some of the time you spend in the car every day and guide the conversation to more of a spiritual tone. All that matters is that we are making a conscious effort to lead our kids in pursuing Christ. We may have never done anything like this or have any clue what we're doing, but isn't that how every other aspect of parenting goes for us anyway?

As much as we teach Christ, we must be Christ to our kids as well. We are the walking, breathing example of

Christian living to our kids, so let them see your faith. Let them see you daily unearthing the riches of God's Word while you sit at the kitchen table in the mornings. Have them tag along when you go to share the gospel with a neighbor or when you go to pray with a friend in need.

Confess your sin when you sin against your kids. I come across students all the time who have no idea how to confess their sins because they have never seen it. We cannot allow the blindness of our pride to hinder us from shepherding our kids. They are watching us and learning from us—for both the good and the bad.

There is no greater honor than to be the living, breathing picture of the loving Father to our kids. We get to mirror the grace He extends to us in our sins. We get to be a refuge for them when their world seems like it is collapsing in on them, just like He was our help in times of trouble. We get to shepherd our kids through life just as He has been the wisdom for us in our lives. We get to love our kids because He has shown us what that paternal love looks like.

The most loving act I can ever do as a dad is to reveal to my kids that there is someone who has loved them more, pursued them harder, and sacrificed everything for them: God Himself. God is the one who entrusted His fearfully and wonderfully made creations to us in the first place; parents are the stewards of this gracious creation of our children. May we see the gracious gift that we have in our children and in turn lead them to the Giver of all that is good. May we chase Christ with all our hearts and be able to lead our families along with us. May we be loving fathers who lead our kids to the Father who loved them first.

CHAPTER 8

Born to Celebrate God's Grace

> "There is a lot to be said about God when
> I get a glimpse of His beauty in this life."

My ever-wise wife told me that this past summer, and it hasn't left me since. It is a phrase that is astonishingly simple but powerfully true. Every single day God makes His invisible attributes known through what He has made (Romans 1:20), and in that we glimpse Hs beauty and grace in tangible ways. We see it in a sunset or a mountaintop view. We taste it in the joy of a little child. It lands on our hearts in the kind words of a stranger.

At times, His glory and grace can be made known at odd moments through surprising means. It is those moments and means that my wife and I have affectionately labeled "measures of grace." We have adopted this little phrase so that we can capture these times when God allows us to taste and see the truths of His Word that He has already written on our hearts.

Take note of these measures of grace for two reasons: first, gratitude. Heather and I don't make the most money in ministry. We don't live in a fancy house or drive brand new cars. Yet God has been gracious to us throughout our lives, and we want to celebrate Him in that. Second, it is part of the way we combat discouragement. It is easy for all of us to remember the hurt we have experienced in our lives, even the smallest cutting words. We don't nearly have the clarity to remember every kind word and moment of peace we have had in our lives. The danger comes as I cling to all my hurt and let much of God's grace roll off my back—I am allowing bitterness to take root in my heart.

We fight our ungrateful hearts by celebrating what God is doing in our lives. This is not a worship of gifts above the Giver Himself; this is the recognition that good gifts come from a gracious God. He is not distant. He is not indifferent to my life. God is with me. God is for me. He is working all things together in my life for His glory. God is constantly stepping into our lives to give us things we did not earn and do not deserve, much like the saving grace He has bestowed on His sons and daughters.

Measures of Grace

There are times in my life when I feel like I have a Job-like call on my life. Every morning spent getting ready in the mirror is the daily reminder of the fact that my two shirt sleeves dangle loosely when everyone else I meet daily does not have that problem. The stares of strangers and their poorly thought-out comments can cut deeply when I least expect it. That is the daily war that goes on in my heart.

Job was a man who had everything—thousands of livestock, a lot of servants, and ten amazing kids. Yet in one moment, Job lost it all. He was utterly heartbroken. In Job 1:20–21 we see Job tear his clothes apart and shave his head. He cries out to God in anguish, but praises His name with the same breath. His circumstances were terrible, but Job chose to focus on the goodness of God.

In Job 2 we see his health fail, and his own wife begs him to curse God and die. Then in the next ten chapters of Job we see a roller coaster of emotions. Job laments the day of his birth because of the heartache and pain he is experiencing. Job's three friends blame Job for everything he has gone through, even though we see Job did not sin in any of this.

He is pressed on every side: physical pain, emotional pain, relational pain, and spiritual anguish. He is hurt and abandoned. He has every excuse to curse God, and yet he does not. As a matter of fact, he hopes in Him even more. As the first part of Job 13:15 says, "Though he slay me, I will hope in him." There is a war of pain and sorrow all around Job, and he still chooses to rest in God. God was still good, even when Job's circumstances were not, and Job wanted to celebrate that goodness even when his pain and his friends told him otherwise.

I can't begin to count the times that God has stepped into the midst of that war in my heart to calm me and encourage me. It is that encouragement that God will send through complete strangers that forms my interesting relationship with those whom I have never met. My expectation toward new people is almost always guarded so that I am prepared for insults or the careless words of others.

However, every once in a while, God will send someone my who that will truly surprise me.

Once I walked into Starbucks to get some writing done. I went to the register to order my usual grande cold brew coffee—black, light ice—and then start typing away on my laptop. Typing with your feet in public almost always elicits some funny reactions from those who pass through to get their daily latte. That is a reaction I am almost always prepared for. That is why I put on my noise-cancelling head-phones, crank a *Citizens & Saints* album, and get to writing. Normally, I can block out what's going on around me and lock in on what I am writing, but that wasn't the case on this particular day.

While I worked, I kept noticing the man at the table right beside me was deeply interested in the fact that I was typing with my feet. He would not go more than a couple of minutes without glancing over to see what I was doing. He seemed like a nice man—he was a well-dressed business-man and appeared to be knocking out emails in between coffee meetings with clients. Seeing that this guy did not seem to be the grouchy type, I decided to make small talk with him in the hope that it could disarm the curiosity around my armlessness. We talked about the weather, Carolina Panther football, and the impending presiden-tial election. It was not until the end of the conversation that I caught the man's name: David. After about ten min-utes of chatting another, client appeared, and I returned to my writing.

Another hour went by, and I was nearly done. David fin-ished his meeting and got up to leave. As he left he plopped a cardboard cup sleeve right in the middle of my table. At first I was mad. I had thought that this nice businessman had stuck me with his trash. In my frustration I stood up to go throw away my newly adopted trash. As I grabbed the sleeve, it fell open to reveal a note inside: "I have really, really been struggling today. I've had verbal abuse from an alcoholic brother all day long. But you have inspired me beyond words. You were a hero today. Thank you for making an old man's day. You inspire me."

I did not see that coming. I had fully intended to come into that coffee shop and block out everything around me so I could knock out some writing, but God had other plans. I had unknowingly become a vessel of God's glory and grace. That man's being encouraged that day had very little to do with my own efforts. I spent just a few minutes interacting with him, but that was all God needed.

The reality is that you never know who is watching you. I knew this guy was glancing at me constantly, but I had no idea what was going on inside of him. I assumed I was just getting stared at, but I had no idea I was being used to encourage a man who was hurting. I can be so blind to the needs of people. I cringe to think how many people I have blindly hurt just by being rude or impatient when I am blowing through my day. Yet, just as easily, how many people see the love of Christ in me in ways beyond my intentions or control?

The measure of grace in that afternoon at Starbucks is that God placed me at that tiny two-seat table for a very specific purpose. God didn't need my preaching ability or for me to shepherd this man in that moment; God needed me to just be there. Living like there is an eternal hope in me was all that I had to do in that moment, and God took care of everything else. It is humbling to know that God is using you to reveal Himself to others and you have no idea. I would have been completely clueless had it not been for that cardboard note that he plopped on my table.

Showing Up in the Stillness

Often the measures of grace in my life aren't as obvious as the clearly expressed encouragement of someone else. God can express His beauty and glory in much more subtle ways, which can easily be skipped over during our busy schedules. I'll be the first person to admit that I go through seasons where I cram my calendar beyond what I truly should. This leaves me running from a meeting to my church office to coffee-shop discipleship in rapid succession. My tight weekly schedule does not afford much margin to go off schedule.

In the seasons of unrelenting busyness, there certainly is no time to stop and smell the roses. I can't help but think what grace I pass by because I am too busy. Sometimes, though, I begin to sense my busyness and I will take some time to get still. I wipe my schedule clean for a day and soak in time with my family. I shove my phone in a drawer with no plan to check it.

God recharges my heart in those times of stillness. It is such a blessing to play tag with my son or to play peek-a-boo with my little girl. I can't begin to count how many beautiful conversations I've had with my wife just by sitting on the couch to take time to catch up. They might be small joys by comparison, but they are measures of grace nonetheless.

Another simple thing that recharges me and reminds me of God's attributes is getting outside and enjoying what His hands have made. I love to take a hike to a mountain peak so that I can see God's creative power for miles in any direction. I will almost sprint up a trail to go see a waterfall. I love being able to see the water dance as it cascades down to the pool below. I love to get up early when I am at the lake just to go down to the dock so that I can absorb the stillness of the morning.

It is the constantly changing beauty of the beach that I love about our family vacations every year. Each summer, as the intensity of student ministry winds down, our family takes a week of vacation at Topsail Island in North Carolina. There is not much to this skinny island: a couple of motels, a handful of restaurants, and a bunch of beach homes, but that is our idea of vacation. We play in the sand and the surf together. I love those moments with my family, but I also love the moments that bracket our fun-filled days. I love being able to wake up early so that I can catch an East Coast sunrise. I love when the kids go to bed and my wife and I can stretch out on the porch with a good book while the surf roars in the background.

This past vacation, one morning I woke up before dawn, grabbed a cup of coffee and Watchman Nee's *The Normal Christian Life*, and went to the porch and read while the sun came up. While I sat in the stillness of that beach morning, God used Nee's words to break my hard and busy heart. Many things Nee describes in the "normal" Christian life seemed very abnormal to me. I'll never forget this quote: "I must first have a sense of God's possession of me before I can have a sense of His presence with me."

That sentence landed on my heart like a hammer. About the only things I had a sense of were how busy and how stressed I was. I folded the book closed and began to confess my lack of rest and my lack of trust before the Father. I sat there in my rocking chair, praying with my eyes open and soaking in the beauty of the morning, which unfolded like an artist's painting.

As the sun started to illuminate the sky, I could start to make out spotty, dark storm clouds that dotted the horizon. The sun began to climb higher as beautiful brushstrokes of color swept across the sky. I had never seen such vivid colors in a sunrise in all my life. Orange, red, pink, purple, and yellow burst through the sky as dark black clouds hung in the foreground. God's beauty and power were on display in such a clear way. God's bold statement of creative presence was my very tangible reminder that He held my life in the same hand which He painted the beautiful brushstrokes of color in that sunrise.

Thirty-six hours later that God reminded me again of His presence. We had just had a strong thunderstorm chase us from the beach back into the beach house. The storm shook our house with thunder and wind for nearly an hour until it abruptly came to a stop. As I sat on the bed with my son watching cartoons, I could see beautiful colors peeking through the blinds.

I stepped out on the back porch to see that the storm had left an exquisite sunset in its wake. I heard my wife yell from the front porch, "Everyone, come look!" I jogged through the house to the front porch to find a double rainbow stretched over the ocean. Our little beach house was bracketed by beauty after this storm. A beauty that we could enjoy because of God's power colliding with our stillness.

God kept piling these measures of grace all throughout our vacation there on Topsail that week. At each little measure, my heart would bounce back to that Watchman Nee quote. I must sense God's possession before I can sense His presence with me. God was breaking my heart over my lack of awareness and gratitude of His working in my life. As a pastor, I have a knowledge-based understanding of His upholding me with His hand. I know the promises of Scripture that He is with me and that He is for me. Yet how many times do I allow my busy schedule to carry me past the evidence of His power and beauty?

How many times have we skipped right by God's grace made manifest? How many people have we walked by who needed the hope that we can give them, but we didn't have the time to give it? Our lives lack the beauty of God because we don't take the time to soak it in. Our lack of sharing the gospel isn't rooted in a lack of missions; it is found in our reluctance to testify to God's grace in our own lives.

Psalm 46:10 may be the most well-known passage on being still before the Lord:

> Be still, and know that I am God.
>   I will be exalted among the nations,
>   I will be exalted in the earth!

This seems easy enough to obey, but, as in the case of many verses, there is more going on here. The kingdoms of the earth have long chased after their desires and glory but now lash out against the throne of David. There is a lot of noise in Psalm 46. All through this chapter we see the earth giving way, waters roaring, mountains trembling, nations raging, and kingdoms tottering. There are the nations of the world rising up against Israel. There must be a sense of fear on Israel's part, given that the world is seeking to lay waste to them.

Amid the fear and the noise there are two commands in the last four verses of Psalm 46. The first comes in verse 8 where God tells His people to "come, behold the works of the Lord," and the second is in verse 10 where the Father proclaims, "be still and know that I am God." In contrast to the action, war and opposition, there is a simple command to sit still and behold the glory of God. In circumstances like that, we may easily skip that command and get to making war against the enemies of God. All the while, the Creator and Sustainer of the universe wants us to sit down. His desire is for us to remember He's got this handled.

Think of Elijah in 1 Kings. God begins Elijah's ministry with a bang. Prophecies of a crippling drought have come to be (17:1–7). Elijah feeds a widow's family for days on end with a single jar of flour and a jug of oil (17:8–16). God uses Elijah to bring the widow's son back to life after sickness fell upon him and he died (17:17–24). God sends fire down onto Mount Carmel in a showdown with 450 prophets of Baal (18:20–40). After the prophets are defeated, Elijah prays and rain again comes upon the land (18:41–46). God uses Elijah in dramatic and unexpected ways.

That is when Ahab tells Elijah that he's coming to take his life. It is this threat that is uttered, even as Mount Carmel still smolders, that strips Elijah of his confidence. He flees for his life into the desert. There under a broom tree Elijah sits down, says he's ready to die, and then goes to sleep. He awakes to an angel of the Lord who feeds him hot bread and water. With this new sustenance, Elijah journeys for forty days to Mount Horeb, the same mountain where Moses received the Ten Commandments, and he hides in a cave.

In this cave the word of the Lord calls Elijah out. He witnesses a wind that shattered mountains, an earthquake, and a fire. Yet 1 Kings 19:11–12 says that the Lord was not in any of those events. Instead, Scripture says Elijah hears a "low whisper" (or a still, small voice) that comes to Elijah. We don't know what, if anything, was said in the whisper, but we see Elijah emboldened and sent out by God to anoint both kings and prophets.

There is plenty of debate over what led Elijah to want to die in the desert or what the still, small voice really was. I don't have much to offer in the way of clarity on either of those points, but there are a few things that stand out in these chapters of 1 Kings. First, Elijah got so busy being a history-altering prophet of God that he lost sight of both his brotherhood of prophets and lost sight of his sustaining Father. Secondly, as he's frustrated and spiritually wounded, God sustains him physically with food and invigorates him in the stillness and sends him out with a new call.

I see many pastors and believers whose lives read much like Elijah's. Sometimes we start doing so much for the kingdom that we lose sight of the King. Our eyes become fixed on how the story of our lives is playing out rather than being fixed on the One who authors that story. We are so busy giving of ourselves that we aren't taking time to savor the One whom we serve. We are so busy feeding others that we begin to spiritually starve ourselves, and before long we find ourselves in a spiritual desert, frustrated and exhausted.

The question comes to the modern believer: do I stop my chaotic life enough to savor the beauty and glory of the One I serve? I've got to make the emphasis of my life more about abiding in God than doing for God. As John 15:4 declares to disciples everywhere, it is only in abiding, or resting, in Him that we bear fruit: "Abide in me, and I in you. As the branch cannot bear fruit by itself, unless it abides in the vine, neither can you, unless you abide in me." It is that fruit that makes God look glorious. As we rest in Him, we obey His commands and show a law that is nothing like human laws. As we rest in His love, we can reflect the disciple's trademark love that a love-starved world craves. It is only as we abide in Him that we have joy to bring to the world.

The church doesn't have a *doing* problem; we have an *abiding* problem. We can't make our Christian identity about what we do, because we then usurp the glory of the very Christ whose name we bear. It is God who works mightily in the hearts of lost people. We are the workers in a field full of those who need to hear the gospel. We have a role to play in being gospel-minded, but God is the One who does the real work. As Paul says in 1 Corinthians 3:7, "Neither he who plants nor he who waters is anything, but only God who gives the growth."

That is why for us as a church, we cannot focus our lives on what we produce above the One for whose purpose we live. That is why we submit to Him as the Lord of our lives. It is for His purposes the we nourish ourselves in His Word—that we may have the strength to stand when trials come. That is why we pray that His will be done and not ours. Ultimately our lives are not about us but about Him.

That is what measures of grace are all about: Him. They are never going to be the source of my spiritual strength or encouragement. They will never be God's lone voice speaking into my life. They are great reminders of the good God I serve. They're the bread crumbs that lead me back to my one true home. They are the visible aspects of God's grace in my life. Those gracious aspects cause me to see and savor my glorious Savior.

May I treasure every single reminder of how remarkable my Heavenly Father is and that in doing so I can celebrate the One in whose image I am fearfully and wonderfully made. May I boast in Him, in His riches, and in His grace. That in living for my Savior and Creator I can be about what He is about: trying to see and save that which is lost.

My Prayer for You

Always love.
Always trust.
Always pray.
Always rejoice.
Always give thanks.

Those words are how I summarize what Paul says to the Thessalonian church at the end of 1 Thessalonians 5. The Thessalonians were a church that loved each other well, followed the example of Christ, and did so in view of the fact of the promised return of Jesus Christ. They made their lives to be about Jesus and nothing else. His grace had carried them this far, and, in "Amazing Grace" fashion, they knew grace would lead them home.

My prayer for you is that you may live every single day in view of that grace. That you would distinctly see God's fingerprints all over your life. He is carrying you along at every stop along the way, and He has not abandoned you. He has an amazing plan for your life—to be about His kingdom and His glory. Think about the words of Jeremiah 29:11–14:

For I know the plans I have for you, declares the LORD, plans for welfare and not for evil, to give you a future and a hope. Then you will call upon me and come and pray to me, and I will hear you. You will seek me and find me, when you seek me with all your heart. I will be found by you, declares the LORD, and I will restore your fortunes and gather you from all the nations and all the places where I have driven you, declares the LORD, and I will bring you back to the place from which I sent you into exile.

Many of us know the words of verse 11, but it is the following three verses that sing out in my heart. His plans for me are centered on Him. Just look at whom all the verbs point to:

> Call upon Me.
> Pray to Me.
> I will hear you.
> Seek Me.
> Find Me.
> I will restore and gather.
> I will bring you back.

His plan for our future is His glory and nothing else. Our circumstances are irrelevant because He is not going to let circumstances stand in the way of His glory. We are called to greater things than our own lives and circumstances. We are to be about our Master's plans and our Master's glory, in every affliction, big or small. May we always seek Him in our joy and sorrow. May we offer Him both our Sundays and our workdays. He deserves for us to center our hearts and our affections on Him. He is the one we call to and trust. It is His grace that leads us, and He is the one our hearts are fixed on.

May that always be true of us, that we pursued Him until our very last breath. We chased, we fought, we loved, and we trusted—until grace leads us home.

LEXHAM PRESS

—

THE TESTING OF A FATHER'S FAITH

In *Shattered Prayers* Kenneth Ching masterfully recounts his battle of struggling to understand God's plan when some prayers are answered and others are not. When his son is born with a rare genetic condition, he learns to rejoice when his son is healthy and grieve when he is sick. This is a story about wrestling with God, about suffering and doubt, and ultimately about the hope that comes only in the midst of brokenness.

"*Shattered Prayers is an artful examination of faith in the face of suffering. In recounting his family's story, Ching allows the reader access to a father's inner dialogue with a candor that is at turns frightening, vulnerable, and beautiful—often at the same time. And while the book's primary preoccupations are questions of faith, the story is told with a sense of drama that keeps the reader rapt.*"
—Gabriel Urza, author of *All That Followed*

—

LexhamPress.com/Shattered-Prayers